LIVING
FROM THE
HEART
Jesus Gave You

15th Anniversary
Study Edition
Revised 2013

James G. Friesen, Ph.D.
E. James Wilder, Ph.D.
Anne M. Bierling, M.A.
Rick Koepcke, M.A.
Maribeth Poole, M.A.

Shepherd's House Inc.
P.O. Box 2376
East Peoria, IL 61611

 A LIFE MODEL™ BOOK

Living from the Heart Jesus Gave You
by James G. Friesen, Ph.D., E. James Wilder, Ph.D.,
Anne M. Bierling, M.A., Rick Koepcke, M.A., and
Maribeth Poole, M.A.

ISBN: 978-1-935629-14-6

Printed by:
Shepherd's House, Inc.
P.O. Box 2376
East Peoria, IL 61611
www.lifemodel.org
www.joystartshere.com

 A LIFE MODEL™ BOOK

Scripture quotations are from The Holy Bible: New International Version,
copyright 1973, 1978, 1984, by the International Bible Society.
Published by Zondervan Bible Publishers, Grand Rapids, Michigan.

Order from www.lifemodel.org

Cover design by The Brandvertisers, Inc.

Acknowledgements

Wanda K. Morgan, Ph.D., from the Shepherd's House Board of Directors, edited this 15th year anniversary edition of *Living From The Heart Jesus Gave You*. This anniversary edition has been rearranged so as to divide the chapters into topics that lend themselves to weekly group studies.

Dr. Morgan has created a special selection of study questions for the fourteen studies in this new version. One of the early groups to divide this book into smaller segments for study groups was the Community of Grace Church in Hayward, California. Their study questions have been used along with other questions provided by Dr. Morgan. Additional study guide materials by Dr. Morgan can be found on www.joystartshere.com. Special thanks to Dr. Morgan and the Community of Grace Church for their contributions.

The text of the original authors of *Living From The Heart Jesus Gave You* has been left intact, with one exception. The early version carried a section on changing fear bonds to love bonds just before the section on maturity. However, maturity has a significant influence on how we go about changing fear bonds to love bonds. For a decade or so we posted an updated version of the "fear bond to love bond" material on the LifeModel.org website. In this book we have inserted the updated version into the text after the discussion of maturity. The original "fear bonds to love bonds" can be found in Appendix A of this book.

Translations

of

Living From The Heart Jesus Gave You

El Gozo Que Restaura
(Spanish)

Viviendo Com O Coração Que Jesus Te Deu
(Portuguese)

Das Life-Model
(German)

Leven Naar Gods Plan
(Dutch)

Vivre Selon Le Cœur Que Jésus Vous A Donné
(French)

Dari Hati Yang Diberikan Yesus
(Indonesian)

Plus:

Korean
Russian
Chinese

Contents

Frequently Asked Questions

What Is Shepherd's House?

Shepherd's House is a Not-For-Profit organization that promotes joyful relationships and recovery skills for the world. Shepherd's House equips existing networks with the skills to thrive rather than creating a large organization or network of our own. We are working to develop a self-propagating model of recovery that will allow people to spread good relationships in low-joy places of the world. Currently, recovery is largely left to people with advanced degrees - a solution that will not spread to most low-joy parts of the world. Since there is little funding to develop self-propagating recovery, we are funding it through providing materials, training and assessment tools. The main model we have developed to direct our work is the Life Model. *Living From The Heart Jesus Gave You* was one of the first books based on the Life Model.

What Is the Life Model?

The Life Model is a unifying approach to ministries of counseling, recovery, pastoral care, prayer ministry, deliverance, inner healing, child rearing, body life and health. The Life Model is a multigenerational model of redemption and maturity from conception to death. While the Life Model incorporates the best in science and medicine, we were careful to create a model that was not based on Western education, but rather on a biblical worldview that is thousands of years old and well tested for the transformation of identity, character and culture.

The Life Model has three distinctive features. First, it depends on a multigenerational community for the formation of maturity. Second, it depends upon an Immanuel lifestyle where God's interactive presence informs all we do and creates "shalom." In shalom, everything is in the right place, at the right time, in the right amount for God and people. The third distinctive feature of the Life Model comes from the specific, learned, relational skills needed for a mature human identity. While everyone is born with the brain wiring needed to be a predator, training in the gentle-protector skills are needed to form godly character. These skills have been identified by brain studies and writings begining about the year 2000. These brain skills are needed in all humans and are only acquired by joyful interactions and relationships with other people who already have the skills.

The absence of key relational skills and maturity are almost always behind failures of ministers, ministries and missions. Sadly, the lacking skills are rarely identified, and when the lack of skill is seen, no one knows how to restore the skill. Relational skills are the basis for expressing godly character and identity to others around us when the "heart Jesus gave us" seeks expression. Consequently, Shepherd's House has developed materials and training to help restore and propagate gentle-protector, relational brain skills.

Our Hope

Our hope is to develop, test and then distribute Life Model technology to as many existing networks as possible. We are planting seeds that will change whole cultures, alter generational heritages and equip people with the skills they need to thrive.

What Is the Life Model Works?

A wide range of Life Model media, training, church programs and study materials have been developed by Shepherd's House that are distributed and managed by the Life Model Works.
- Books
- Videos
- JOYStream conferences on-line
- JIMTalks audio on the biblical basis for the Life Model
- On-line courses
- Connexus for a thriving community
- THRIVE skill training for mentors and leaders
- JoyStartsHere.com

History of The Life Model

1971 • Shepherd's House Inc. is founded with the primary purpose of using Christian counseling principles to help people with their emotional and spiritual needs.

1980s • Shepherd's House provides nearly 1,200 monthly counseling appointments with women who had been sexually abused as children.

1990s • Insurance industry calculates the cost for recovery of one sexually abused child to be $15 million. Realizing a more affordable solution is needed, Counselor Jane Willard introduces healing prayer. Through these changes the Shepherd's House staff begin developing a new model that comes to be called the *Life Model*.

2002 • Shepherd's House staff identifies nineteen relational brain skills. The THRIVE training team headed by Chris and Jen Coursey develops ways for ordinary people to identify lacking skills and train others in these brain skills.

2008 • Shepherd's House works with Dr. Karl Lehman of Chicago to develop the Immanuel Prayer Process, combining healing prayer and cutting-edge neuroscience to facilitate trauma resolution in large-group settings. Initial tests in Colombia and Sri Lanka yield positive outcomes for self-propagating recovery. Further testing and research awaits funding.

2009 • Ed Khouri and Jim Wilder develop a trauma and addiction recovery program called *Thriving* (now called *Connexus for a thriving community)*, serves as a test program for self-propagating recovery as a normal function of the local church. Further development awaits additional funding.

2011 • Shepherd's House celebrates 40 years of helping people thrive.

2013 • *Joy Starts Here* book and joy-planting movement begins with a special focus on the three places life is formed: home, school and church. See joystartshere.com to participate and spread joy.

What Is Our Dream?

We want to see self-propagating recovery as the normal function of the church around the world. We wish to see people of joy who actively start joy where it is needed in every low-joy corner of life.

The Challenge

As evil spreads through any community or group, it leaves behind signs such as trauma, but even more insidiously, it brings about the disappearance of relationships, trust and love. The basic skills necessary for joyful relationships weaken and disappear from one generation to the next. The abuse, violence and damage spread from person to person without help. One in three abused children grows up to be an abuser. In the case of pedophiles, each one will abuse about 260 children. Two-thirds of addicts report being abused as children, and the children of addicts are three times more likely to be abused. At Shepherd's House we have seen first-hand how, when this evil spreads, everyone suffers. Not only do trauma and addictions cause much suffering, they also produce damaging changes in the brain. Until now there has only been one solution.

The Existing Solution

The clinical solutions currently are expensive and cumbersome; they require extreme levels of education and do not spread on their own. Even those people who are able to benefit from modern treatments are not able to then help others without undergoing the same extensive training that therapists need. From a global perspective, factors such as wars, AIDS, societal disintegration, child abuse, violent crime, human trafficking, addictions, and terrorism have left about a quarter of the world's population showing significant signs of trauma. Against such overwhelming circumstances, our current recovery systems end up looking like a Band-Aid on a volcano. Shepherd's House solutions make it possible for ordinary people to pass on to others what they have learned, without extensive training.

Solution #2 - Self-propagating Recovery

Along with transferable training, Shepherd's House is committed to self-propagating recovery that transforms cultures. The Christian church is the only global force whose calling is to love and reach even those who see them as enemies.

If we are able to develop an effective self-propagating recovery program, the best existing distribution system for global recovery would be the relational network created by the church. All over the world, most new converts to Christianity come from backgrounds of trauma and/or addiction. They enter into the church having impaired maturity and relational skills. Simple conversion does not provide the missing brain skills they need for healthy relationships, any more than salvation will make them suddenly literate.

Thus the church faces the recovery problem both inside its congregations and in its mission. In the past, the church has shown a capacity to change cultures, although it lacks that vital function in most of the Western world at this time. In spite of this current state, we at Shepherd's House are dreaming of a self-propagating recovery model that could change cultures through the ordinary life of the church. We believe that we are on that path.

The Solution Needs to be Distributed

The Life Model shows promise as a solution that is both high-tech in its foundations and low-tech in its implementation, that ordinary Christians can use without specialized education. Elements have already been shown to work in groups, and the results demonstrate self-propagation.

The remaining elements exist conceptually in the minds of an aging but devoted group at Shepherd's House. While self-propagating healing is easier to do through the Immanuel Process, self-propagating relational skills are not as easy to transfer. The relational skills take community, bonded relationships and time. The Shepherd's House staff believes this model and the skills it teaches could reduce and even prevent some trauma and addiction, as well as provide healing and improve relationships.

Relational Joy and the Life Model

The Life Model has spread quietly to many Christian groups: Evangelical, Anglican, Coptic, Roman Catholic, Eastern Rite Catholic, Holiness, Arminian, Wesleyan, Calvinist, Savationist, Pietist, Reformed, Lutheran, Messianic, Anabaptist, Brethren, Apostolic, emergent, Pentecostal, Mennonite, Vineyard, YWAM and Baptist to name a few. The Life Model is endorsed by none of these groups, but all find help in a model built on the fundamental bonds that transform those who receive abundant life through Christ.

The Life Model has found a place in missions, healing ministries, recovery ministries and schools. The late Dr. Dallas Willard used *Living From The Heart Jesus Gave You* as a textbook in seminary classes and said, "The Life Model is the best model I have seen for bringing Christ to the center of counseling and restoring the disintegrating community fabric within Christian churches." The Life Model itself developed with Dr. Willard's influence through his wife Jane, who was a long term Shepherd's House staff member.

Governments, prisons, schools and leaders from high-trauma places like Sudan, Colombia, Nigeria and Southeast Asian nations have invited the Life Model into their situations. Atheists, Jews, Muslims and people from many persuasions, who want to be fully alive, have been attracted to the Life Model for joyful relationships, peaceful resolution of life's hurts, belonging with others and transformed character.

Relational joy is at the heart of the Life Model. Gentle-protector brain skills, Immanuel awareness of God with us, transformation of character, growth of maturity, nurturing a multigenerational community, recovery from trauma, development of resilience, prevention of predatory personality development and hope for the low-joy places of the world all require relational joy. Are you in?

Relational joy starts with knowing who we really are meant to be, when we see ourselves and then others through the awareness and discernment of the heart Jesus gives us. Let us discover together how to live from the heart Jesus gave you.

Elements of the Problem That Require Elements in a Solution

- Trauma and addictions change our identities; therefore the solution must also change identities.
- Trauma self-propagates; therefore the solution must self-propagate.
- Trauma blocks the development of maturity and character; therefore the solution must restore maturity and godly character.
- Trauma encourages people to reject others; therefore the solution must create belonging.
- Trauma and addictions spread without needing education; although the solution should be based on the best science, it should not require a Western education or medical model.
- Violence and terrorism traumatize whole groups at once; therefore the solution must heal whole groups at once.
- All human cultures, races and ethnicities have the same nervous systems and the same spiritual needs. A solution based on solid neurology and Biblical spirituality would be a solution as universal as the causes for trauma.
- The recovery model must be high-tech design with a low-tech implementation.
- Abuse usually spreads through unhealthy relationships. The 19 relational brain skills, taught through THRIVE materials in bonded relationships, train and encourage people towards joyful relating.
- The identities formed by the solution must match God's design for us.

How Can I Join The Joy-starter Movement?

You can find the joy-starting movement at JoyStartsHere.com, and we can reach our dream together.

LIVING FROM THE HEART
JESUS GAVE YOU

Who Should Read This

This book is for the *leaders* of the church and for the *wounded* in the church community.

First, we target the leaders because any strong Christian leader needs to know how to serve. In order to serve, a leader needs to understand people and how easily their hearts are wounded. Jesus made it His number one mission to serve people. He talked with them, walked with them, ate with them, and stayed with them. He knew about their wounds, and literally gave His life to heal their broken hearts. He was the Leader of all leaders, and our leaders are to follow His example and sacrificially serve the weak and wounded.

We also write to the wounded. This is a group that has been long overlooked and horribly ignored. We are deeply concerned because this has resulted in the rejection of many beautiful souls and in the decline of the church at large. You will find as you work through this book that *Living From The Heart Jesus Gave You* promotes a different atmosphere, one where the wounded are valued as persons who can contribute to the on-going life of the church.

At Shepherd's House our heartfelt desire is to see church communities become more effective. In order to learn what churches are doing that is effective in helping wounded people, we conducted research with a selected sample of churches nationwide. We found that when they set aside monies and created programs for wounded people, those programs eventually got drained and died. *But, when churches embraced and pulled wounded people into the center of strong families, a surprising phenomenon called "synergy" developed.* Synergy is what happens when two agents are combined, and they increase each other's effectiveness. People are energized to new levels in the church when the weak and the strong are combined. The church needs the wounded, and wounded hearts need the church. And synergy develops most powerfully when both of these groups are living from the hearts Jesus gave them.

Where You Are Headed

You are somewhere on your path to maturity. There will, undoubtedly, be unforeseen difficulties, and you still have a way to go, but do not be discouraged because your destination is better than you can even imagine right now.

Your journey will go well if you can live from your heart, "the heart Jesus gave you," as Dr. Dallas Willard would say. While you are living from your *hurt*, you may not be able to discover the characteristics of your *heart*. As God heals the hurt and is invited into every area of your life, you will be able to discover the nature of your heart. The people who see you as God sees you can tell you what your heart is really like, so pay attention to what they tell you about your heart and use it as your guide for living. When you are living from your heart you are truly being yourself. Joy increases and fear decreases, as you go about your daily activities. The word "freedom" is often used to describe how it feels to live from your *heart*, and you certainly need freedom to make headway along your maturity pathway.

And while you are on that pathway, try to avoid isolation. You cannot overcome life's obstacles alone. As your maturity progresses, you will be able to help others discover how to live from their hearts, too. That is a fulfilling experience. You can be incredibly proud of those you have helped in making progress with maturity, and that will give you increased confidence that your own journey is on its proper course. You will find that others are growing as you are growing.

Experiencing God, loving one another, and bearing each other's burdens will become richer and more natural as you learn more about receiving and giving life. *Living From The Heart Jesus Gave You* is about receiving and giving life, reaching a higher level of maturity, receiving healing for life's inevitable traumas, and having your life governed by the joy of the Lord. But this process does not happen in isolation. It takes family and it takes community, as you will learn in the pages ahead.

CHAPTER

1

WHOLENESS

People need to know who they are. They also need to be reminded who they are, frequently, by those who love them, and really know them. And they need repair, so that they can live from the hearts Jesus gave them. That is what it takes to achieve wholeness in a fractured world. It takes belonging to a community. It takes a whole lot of work in the area of maturity. It takes God's hand to boost people when they are stuck, and it takes a lifetime.

There are many essential components to becoming whole. Belonging to a family, receiving and giving life, recovering from the effects of traumas and contributing to a community. These are a few of the factors that help people learn who they really are. But when there are deficiencies in any of these areas, people remain stuck and do not learn to live from their hearts – their true God-given identities.

Why We Need Counselors

There would be no need for counseling except for the damage caused to all people by sin and the fall. Since then all creation has groaned and no human being has grown straight and true, according to God's design, except for God's only begotten son Jesus. Through Jesus we have the salvation that will finally correct all the damage of sin. This salvation works among us directly through God's activities and indirectly through His people—the people of God—His church. Because God does not intend His salvation to simply be a ticket into Heaven, we His followers must participate with Him in overcoming the results of sin in our day-to-day existence here on earth. This change of our hearts and lives is the work of sanctification and redemption. Once saved through repentance and the forgiveness of our sins, we must return to living life as though God's Kingdom has come and His will is being done on earth as it is in Heaven. Far too often we have seen our salvation as something that takes effect after this life not a way of life that extends into eternity. Here on earth there is work to be done and God expects us to do it. Our work will not save us but it will express that we are new creations. It is our work to grow and reach maturity together with all the saints. To achieve this we must live from our new hearts, being sanctified, healed, delivered from evil and guided by God alone. We are both saved and being saved.

The godly counselor, just like all mature believers, participates with God in helping others put their lives right again—the day-to-day expression of our salvation. Traumas, as we will refer to them here, are the wounds (or injuries) left in our identities that render us less than what God had in mind when He created us. Traumas block growth. Traumas block or slow proper maturity. Traumatic wounds can be caused by adding something to us we should not have--just as a bullet adds its effect to a body it encounters. Traumatic injuries can be caused by the absence of what the soul needs--just as malnutrition can cripple the body. Traumas not only cause injury and pain, traumas block or slow the process of maturity. When the traumatized person is very young this blocked or slowed maturity can cripple, disfigure or prevent the growth of proper maturity or normal faculties of identity. When maturity is slow or blocked always look for these two types of trauma.

Sin adds to our lives what should not be there and subtracts what should be from three sources: the world, the flesh and evil spirit beings. Sin always blocks maturity. Christian counseling must address these evils but not in human strength, not by human wisdom, and not by human plans. This is the work of God's redemption and He alone is worthy to direct and achieve His divine purpose in our salvation. This work can only be accomplished by life in the Spirit through hearts that are alive to God. Too often, pastors, counselors and churches attempt to plan, direct, control and make programs of God's salvation. The results are what we would expect of the flesh at work.

There is a third problem that counselors must address. Not only must they follow God's leading to remove that which blocks or hinders growth and holiness, add that which is lacking for complete and full life in the Spirit, but counselors must address misdirected growth. Jim Wilder has in his home three small trees planted together, whose trunks were braided together while they were young and supple. In the same way people may mature in crooked ways because those who guide their growth chose a twisted path for them to follow. Perhaps they were given a bad example of what a man, woman, father, mother or Christian should be. Perhaps they were taught to laugh at those who weep, curse those who curse them, to get revenge on those who betray them, drink with their friends every Saturday or holiday, lust after many women or other men, control others with threats or anger when they don't get their way and these habits have grown so long and so deep that they have become their character. Surely this is not how God meant us to grow.

The godly counselor seeks to remove that which is unseemly and even deadly from the lives of those whom he shepherds, to add their lives the missing vitamins and nutrition for their souls and spirits and to produce healthy maturity even where the beginnings were crooked and evil.

To this misguided growth the Christian pastor or counselor must apply instruction in the word of God to reveal its error and God's true desire for our growth. Repentance, confession, forgiveness then lead to healing, deliverance and spiritual relationships with God and his people where prayer, praise, worship and the fruit of the Spirit begin to form godly character. Now true maturity can begin its growth—but maturity only grows in the fellowship of God's family.

Having removed the two blocks to maturity and addressed the misguided maturity that has already grown though the leading of God's Spirit at work in his or her heart, the Christian counselor is now ready to begin the human part of counseling—directing, guiding, encouraging, supplying what is lacking for the growth of true maturity. This is obviously work for the mature believer in the context of a growing church fellowship. For true maturity to grow every aspect of the Christian life, every provision of God for our redemption, every teaching of Scripture, every nudge of the Holy Spirit must be given free and full expression. To this we add our full commitment and effort--our whole heart, soul and strength.

Immaturity is addressed as a problem in 1 Corinthians 3:1-3 and Hebrews 5:11-14 while in Ephesians 4:11-15 we are told that the gifts of Jesus that "some should be apostles, some prophets, some evangelists, some pastors and teachers, for the equipping of the saints, for the work of ministry, for building up the body of Christ, until we all attain to the unity of the faith, and of the knowledge of the Son of God, to **mature** manhood, to the measure of the stature of the fullness of Christ, so that we may **no longer be children**... we are to **grow up in every way** into him who is the head, into Christ." Thus the gifts of Jesus are the people in His body that will bring His body to maturity, to grow up in **every way**. Then we will be "perfect and complete, lacking in nothing" (James 1:4b) and this completeness, James tells us comes from the steadfastness born of trials. Indeed, we are to "count it all joy, my brethren, when you meet various trials, for you know that the testing of your faith produces steadfastness." (verses 2-3) It is this very mystery of how trauma becomes joy, steadfast character and a maturity that is complete, lacking nothing that we will examine in this little book. This path is the one that Christian counselors must learn to know well so the body as well as each member can "grow up in every way into him who is the head, even into Christ."

The popular advice is to work it out in therapy. After all, getting people through life's sticking points is supposed to happen in therapy.

Therapy Is Not Enough

But what often happens in traditional therapy? Confidentiality forms are brought out. Clients are told this is a place to speak honestly. They are told that once they learn to be honest, and open up in the therapist's office, they will be able to open up "out there." However, it does not help people to speak honestly if they live in a world where that is punished. If people learn to authentically share how discouraged they are, how they have a deep longing to connect with others, or how they suffer because of unresolved conflicts, they risk being punished "out there." It does no good to be honest about one's suffering in a therapist's office if that is the only arena where it is permitted. Therapy will fail if the client is restricted to being real and honest only in the therapist's office.

The shortcomings of therapy are becoming easier to recognize, as our culture moves farther away from the community-based life we used to enjoy. Therapy seems to work pretty well when clients belong to a community where their lives are nurtured. In a life-giving community, people can usually muster enough energy to move through life's sticking points. They can forge an identity based on the hearts with which they were created, and they can collect the power to live from their hearts. However, it is a challenge in our modern world to create a caring community experience, and when that fails, therapy alone will not succeed.

One striking problem with therapy occurs when the therapist plays the role of the "perfect" person, and the client is supposed to be "imperfect". The truth is, therapists face life's difficulties, too, but many are trained to *play the role* of a therapist, which means they are not supposed to acknowledge their own struggles. Some therapists are trained to know about life, but are not supposed to participate in life during "therapy time" – just play the role of a therapist. In cases where a therapist is only playing a role, therapy will not be life-giving. It takes courage to be an authentic therapist, and that is the foundation of successful therapy.

To be authentic is to be willing to acknowledge how things really are. As one person in a home Bible study group put it, "Isn't it surprising how many people have problems?!" Yes, it is. But perhaps it should not be so surprising. After all, we all must face the same challenges in life. To live authentically is to honestly confront the challenges that we all face. We all are broken. We all face woundedness, dividedness, isolation, and oppression.

People enter therapy seeking to know who they are and how they can receive life. Therapy can nudge them in the right direction, but it cannot tell them who they are and it will not give them life, *unless* the arenas in which they live – including their home, work and church – genuinely support their therapeutic work. Even though therapy can help people face the places that are stuck in their lives, it alone will not supply the power to get them unstuck. *A family and a community need to supply some of the power.* That is where people are supposed to find out who they are, and where they are supposed to find help in getting unstuck. It is where they should receive life.

Sometimes, however, the biological family of origin has been unhelpful or even detrimental in this process. When this is the case, we believe it is God's plan to bring spiritual family members into a person's life. These are family members who will become life-giving in ways that were not provided by the biological family. This godly provision is discussed in Chapter 4 under the subheading, "Spiritual Adoption." At this point it is important to clarify that *The Life Model* does not require people to return to chaotic, dismissive, or abusive families in their attempts to get unstuck. Rather, we pray that God will help us each to discover whom He has in mind to be the life-giving people in our extended spiritual family.

Family and Community Can Fail

Why does community not work as it once did? What is it about today's world that pulls us away from those around us, and pushes us into isolation?

- Hours and hours in front of the television set
- Many more hours on the computer
- Close friends and family moving away
- Neighbors remaining strangers, not friends
- Churches calling themselves the family of God but not acting like it
- Nobody dropping by to share moments of unexpected joy
- No one to help with a crisis
- Food being gulped with precious little time to talk
- Family members eating separately and not sharing mealtimes
- Urgency about getting many things done "now"
- Maintaining a hectic schedule that allows no free time
- Parents feeling overwhelmed with too many commitments

These are each distancing factors that work against people who want a life-giving community, where people care about each other and show it – people who are developing bonds of love. The loss of a caring community has created a nationwide identity crisis. People need to be taught who they are by the community in which they grow up. A family and a community are intended to connect people to each other in loving relationships, which helps them discover who they are. In the absence of life-giving family relationships, promoted by a God-centered community, people continue their unsuccessful search for their God-given identities. They desire to live from their hearts, but do not know how. Instead, their lives are directed by their hurts.

For example, a woman may have unhealed sexual traumas that prevent her from trusting men. If her community fails to repair her wounds, and fails to surround her with trustworthy people, including safe men, she will stay stuck in unsatisfying relationships. Her heart may be sensitive and caring, but she will not be able to get in touch with her sensitivity and caring while she is still living in her pain. When family and community encourage people to face their traumas and get through life's sticking points, they find out who they are. They learn to live from their hearts.

People Need People to Recover

Three professional experiences punctuated this truth for Anne Bierling. When she was the assistant principal and spiritual director at a Christian high school, she was invited to participate in a national task force studying how students grow in their faith. The results of the study concluded that a student's faith is most impacted by being in an authentic relationship with a godly teacher, coach, parent, or adult. Two years later, when she joined the Shepherd's House staff, she learned that 25 years of clinical experience with wounded clients had led them to conclude that people heal in authentic, God-centered relationships and families – and people without these resources recovered much more slowly, if at all. Two years later when she was asked to participate on a leadership team led by a national church consultant, she learned that people *come to the Lord* most readily in fulfilling Christian relationships. Thus, there is a need for everything from the parking lot design to the adult Sunday School classes to cultivate the formation of authentic relationships.

Three professional experiences – one striking conclusion: Students *grow in their faith through relationships, wounded people heal in relationships, and unbelievers come to the Lord through relationships.*

Growth, repair, maturity, and faith development are all intimately tied to relationships. *People do need people* to achieve wholeness in a fractured world.

God's Part and Our Part

It is obvious to most Christians that people need God in order to recover. Yet, it can get complicated – and certainly messed up – when Christians confuse what is God's work and what is ours.

His work includes all the redemptive areas. Salvation, sanctification, deliverance, healing and spiritual adoption are all "God territory". While we may be used as important vessels in these endeavors, God is the only one who can ultimately save us, sanctify us, deliver us from evil, and spiritually adopt us into the appropriate family. When we let God do His work, things happen rather perfectly. But when we presumptuously take over His territory, things tend to crumble all so quickly.

Now the job of maturity is quite another matter. While God is certainly instrumental in guiding and blessing our maturation, it is our job, bestowed upon us way back in the garden, to mature. Maturity is not a spiritual gift nor is it a by-product of salvation. It is something we as Christians must work on our entire lives.

God's jobs – our job. Life becomes more productive when we let God run His territory and we take responsibility to mature ours.

Heart, Soul, and Mind Work Together

When the Word of the Lord tells us to love God with our "heart, soul, and mind" (Matthew 22:37), that includes our whole self. The *heart* is your eyes for seeing spiritual reality (Ecclesiastes 11:9); literally, the heart is the "eyes and ears that know God." The heart is where understanding resides, and is the origin of spiritual discernment. It is particularly influential in shaping a person's sense of spiritual identity. "Living from the heart Jesus gave you" is a term that brings identity together with the spiritual reality of who we are. It is a term that says God designed each of us to be a particular kind of person, with characteristics uniquely our own. When we are living from the heart Jesus gave us, we are being the persons He specifically designed. Living this way integrates the *soul*, where the feelings are, and the *mind*, where the thinking takes place.

In talking about our hearts, we need to be careful to note that the heart is not the emotions. Living from our hearts is not simply doing what our feelings tell us. That would be folly. Living from our hearts means that there is an inner directive that, if governed by the Spirit of God, keeps us on a path that is spiritually attuned to who we are and how God is leading. When our hearts are focused on God, we see who we are and know what we are to be doing. The Word of God reminds us that we all had desperately sick hearts (Jeremiah 17:9), and we all need God to heal them. The heart from Jesus is a reborn heart, a heart where He resides. There are many references to a transformed heart throughout scripture. One passage is in the book of Ephesians, where the apostle Paul prays for the new believers in the Ephesian church. "I pray that out of his glorious riches he may strengthen you with power through his Spirit in your inner being, so that Christ may dwell in your hearts through faith" (Eph. 3:16-17). God wants to live in our hearts. When He is there we experience the freedom and power to be the persons He created us to be.

How To Use These Lessons

These study questions are provided for each section of the book to facilitate both individual study and group discussion of the materials presented.

Suggested Guidelines For Group Discussions

1. Group discussion tends to work best if the group is not smaller than 5 or larger than 10. A larger group can break into consistent smaller groups for the discussion time.
2. The group should have a consistent starting and ending time. This can include worship or fellowship time, but allow the same time each week for the group discussion.
3. It is important for members to commit to attend all sessions and to come prepared, having read the material and answered the questions for the week.
4. Group leaders can evaluate the questions based on the characteristics of their group. Leaders can choose to not discuss any question they see as not appropriate or add any questions of their own that would be helpful for their group.
5. Remind the group weekly that it is important to respect that each person is at his or her own place of growth. For some, the most appropriate choice may be not to share specific parts of their story at this time.

6. Remind the group weekly of need for confidentiality so that group members will not share with others outside the group any personal information shared in the group.

There are three levels of participation available:

1. An individual can read the book on his/her own and complete the questions at the end of each section.
2. A group can read the book together. They would read one section each week and complete the questions provided in a separate journal. The group would meet for an hour and a half (or what ever the group agrees to) to share their answers, observations and life experiences.
3. The most complete study involves using added resources that are provided free on line at joystartshere.com. Resources provided include:
    *   a group leader guide for each book section, formatted for a two hour meeting.
    *   supplemental handouts that expand on some of the significant concepts in more detail than they are covered in the book.
    *   supplemental handouts that cover concepts that are not covered in the book.
    *   an interactive assessment of the characteristics of your true heart.
    *   directions for assembling a study notebook for each group leader and for each group member.
    *   suggested follow up study resources for the group.

LESSON

$$\boxed{1}$$

WHOLENESS
Part 1

1. What has been your experience with the relationships and interactions between the weak and the strong in the church? What is your explanation for this? Pg 1-2
2. If you choose to isolate during this study, what opportunities will you miss? In what ways might you isolate? What are some ways can you avoid isolation as you go through this study? Pg 3
3. Counselors must address three things in people's lives: 1) their traumas, 2) their sin, and 3) their misdirected growth. Describe how each hinders a person from being all God designed them to be. Pg 6-9
4. What factors does a life-giving community add to the healing process that therapy alone cannot supply? Pg 10-11
5. Why do we need a community to help us discover who we are? What happens when people do not experience life-giving community? Pg 12-13
6. Why do you think God uses people to help us grow, recover, and come into a relationship with Him? How has this applied to you personally? Pg 12-13
7. Describe what is "God's part" and what is "our part" in the process of recovery and healing? Pg 13-14
8. What is your reaction to discovering more about the unique heart Jesus gave you and how to live more fully from it?

Wholeness Is Not Achieved Quickly

It has been said that God is not the great magician – He is the great physician. That saying addresses a question which people need to think about clearly – whether fixes from God are always "quick." People typically seek the quickest way out of pain, which is understandable. Pain, of course, demands immediate attention. A more mature approach, however, is to seek God's redemption in the middle of the pain, asking Him to bring healing into our wounds – which can be a much slower process. God does His work in us, pointing us toward wholeness, even while we are in pain. But it is not simply His work; it is our work too. It takes maturity and tenacity on our part to achieve wholeness, and that means persistently dealing with our pain.

There may be times when we are not in a place where we are free from pain, but we can still experience God's amazing redemption. An often-quoted passage in II Corinthians 12 describes how the apostle Paul learned a key lesson. When he was stuck with a tormenting problem which did not go away, even though he pleaded with the Lord three times, he got an answer he was not looking for: God works through weakness. What a profound discovery – he learned to *delight* in "weaknesses, in insults, in hardships, in persecutions, and in difficulties." The good news of the Gospel is that God wants to be with us in the middle of our struggles. That is precisely when He exercises His strength in us. Paul learned to let God be in charge, and to stop asking God to end his hardship. God's strength flowed through him because Paul stopped trying to be in control. He let God take over, and God was able to use him more effectively. Paul could *delight* in suffering because he found it was an opportunity for God's strength to work through him.

Central to the Christian experience is an unchanging belief that God is at work in all things for the good of those who love Him (Romans 8:28), and that means *all* things. He is particularly at work when we are stuck in pain that seems to be endless and meaningless. The time-honored Christian approach to pain and wholeness involves our activity as well as God's: *His work in us is to bring redemption to all of the traumas that have broken us, and our work is to strive for maturity as we progress to wholeness.* The word "redemption" is sometimes difficult to understand, simply because it is used in so many contexts. Here is the way it is used in the *Life Model*: Redemption is God bringing good out of bad, leading us to wholeness, and the experience of God's amazing power. *Redemption means that out of our greatest pain, can come our most profound personal mission in life.*

The biblical understanding of wholeness is succinctly described in the first chapter of James. We are instructed there to consider it *pure joy* whenever we are in the middle of suffering, because that will lead to wholeness. Suffering tests our faith and builds our endurance, so that we can be mature and complete – not divided, but whole. James cautions that we must ask God for wisdom during this stormy process. It takes *total faith* to believe that God will bring us through the storms, or we will be unable to "receive anything" from God; without total faith in God we remain "double-minded" – divided (verse 8). Wholeness comes as we let Him lead us through the storms. We are to welcome suffering because it brings down the walls in our fragmented life so that we can become mature and complete (verse 4). It is God's intent to bring redemption to the wounded and fragmented places in our lives so that our weaknesses can be transformed into strengths. That can happen when we honestly address our pain. Suffering can lead to wholeness if we embrace it. It will take endurance and time, but the benefits are well worth it.

Getting Past What Is In The Past

Some Christians say we should "forget about pain and do what the Bible says – put the past behind us." Everyone agrees it is good to find resolution for past pain, but putting pain behind us is not what the Bible is talking about in the third chapter of Philippians, which is the "putting the past behind us" passage that is usually quoted. Paul's concern there is with boasting about one's personal achievements. He writes that he has reason to boast, but wants to put his *past achievements* behind him. He now considers them worthless, "compared to the unsurpassed greatness of knowing Christ, and the power of his resurrection, [and] the fellowship of sharing in his sufferings" (verse 10). Paul is *not* trying to say people can short-cut dealing with past pain in this passage. Christians are being urged in Paul's strongest language to let nothing hinder them from knowing Christ better, and he specifically includes that suffering will be a part of that.

Recovering from traumas is often difficult, but cannot be ignored. It often takes some focused work, guided by people who have been trained and are experienced. Trauma recovery is the essential task of therapy. Discovering the specific nature of a person's wound is necessary, so that the correct approach for its healing can be chosen. Traumas fall into two distinct categories: *Type A traumas are the absence of good things we all need.* These traumas produce problems in relationships, so recovery requires a loving relationship to repair the Type A wound. *Type B traumas are bad things that should never happen.* They create fear. The "bad events" need to be revisited and the fear needs to be deactivated, so that life can proceed without the fear. Chapter 3 is a fuller introduction to trauma recovery, but it is important to mention at this point how crucial it is to direct recovery efforts according to the type of trauma that is involved. *If the treatment does not fit the particular wound, recovery will not take place.* Type A trauma recovery means sustained love relationships must be available, which give the traumatized person a chance to get unstuck in maturity. Developing trust and letting deep feelings emerge are the building blocks of intimate relationships, and they facilitate maturity. This cannot be expected to take place quickly. It takes both time and a loving family. Recovery from Type B traumas can also take time, even though prayer-centered therapy can speed healing. For both types of traumas the emphasis must be placed on resolution, not on speed. It is the *resolution* of a wound that "puts it in the past," and that requires enough maturity to embrace the wound and invite God's healing.

Christians correctly see that God wants us to put the past behind us, so that we will have nothing stopping us from experiencing His love in this world. A simplistic way of seeing this is just to overlook past pain and to stay focused on the present and future. This is serious denial, and will certainly fail. One client pointed out why this does not work. She said that when the pain from the past is unresolved, she struggles with it every day – it is *not past at that moment*, it is *present. Pain from the past cannot stay in the past, until it receives healing.* The idea needs to be highlighted here, that recovery from traumas is necessary. Past pain is not past until it is resolved enough to end the person's present struggle. Loving relationships and reworking of bad events are essential to help with Type A and Type B traumas, respectively. With God's guidance and power, trauma recovery goes well. God heals and redeems, but it takes more than generally "claiming the victory" over the past. It takes interventions directed appropriately to the trauma wound, or the pain will remain a stumbling block in the present.

A client at Shepherd's House wrote this striking analogy to depict how denying the past had crippled her. Not dealing with the

past had blocked her relationships with others, even with God, and
led to a painful time of isolation.

> My life was a garden of weeds, the beauty of joy and innocent
> youth long since choked out by reality. Then I heard the Word
> of God. The seeds He scattered through my garden sprang up
> beautiful and lush, full of the joy and love that only Christ can
> bring. My garden was a new creation.
>
> But I wasn't tending my garden. I simply thought that it
> would grow and flourish. Then, quite without warning, the
> flowers began to die. Not many at first, so that one might
> hardly notice. But then the gaps grew larger, like holes in a
> beautiful carpet. Others visiting my garden may have noticed
> when it began, but no one was invited in. They could only
> look from the gate, where perfection could be perceived.
>
> Within those holes the problem is clearly seen. All of the
> weeds were still there. The garden had grown up around and in
> spite of them, but there they were choking and destroying the
> beauty once again.
>
> Then began the cooling of my love for the Lord. I may not
> ever have invited Him into my garden, simply allowing the
> seeds to be scattered over the fence. I didn't talk to Him any
> more, didn't go to His house any more, and didn't read His
> letters any more . . . and I am alone without Him. Only I can
> unlock the gate so that He can enter and help me identify and
> remove the weeds so that life can flourish once again. [All cli-
> ent information is used with permission.]

We dare not try to just "forget about pain" or it will block us
from connecting to God and to the family He has given us. We
may try to disconnect from pain in small ways at first. For example,
we may intentionally stay very busy so we don't have to get in touch

with *any* feelings. However, being too busy means we lose friends. Eventually, we end up completely isolated if we avoid working on our pain. Only when we *embrace the pain* will we be successful at putting it in the past, so that we can be more effective in getting closer to others, including God.

Achieving Wholeness in a Fractured World

The world is broken – nothing at all like the finely tuned place God created. The same can be said of us – we are broken and fallen. There is a war in progress between the prince of fallen angels and the Creator, and spiritual battles are frequent and widespread. None of us can escape the effects of the spiritual warfare. We are all vulnerable, and the world fractures us in many ways throughout our lives. Consequently, we are unable to avoid traumas, some of which leave long-lasting scars.

Particularly when they come during childhood, traumas can have profoundly detrimental effects. Even careful parents cannot keep children completely out of harm's way. Kids will be traumatized one way or another, and many people spend much of their adult lives trying to overcome the effects of the early traumas. *Trying to overcome the effects of the early traumas* is usually not recognized as such, because it takes the form of struggling through life, reading the latest self-improvement books, and feeling stuck with an annoying bad habit. These are attempts to change the *trauma effects* without looking at the *trauma that produced the effects*. This is a major problem, not only because the efforts for self-improvement fail if they are misdirected, but also because the widespread existence of child abuse is seriously overlooked.

Study after study finds the same compelling conclusion. About a third of us have been traumatized as children in the form of physi-

Building Joy

Building joy means getting closer to God and to people. While it is a very authentic process that cannot be fabricated, here are some "joy-building" ideas to first practice with our families and then extend to the wounded community.

1. Smile whenever you greet those you love, and use sincere voice tones.

2. Ask questions that invite others to tell you truthfully how they are doing, and what they are thinking. Listen intently without interrupting.

3. Take a sincere interest in really knowing the other person. Work hard to understand the other's fears, joys, passions, talents and pain.

4. Treat each other with dignity and respect. When ending a discussion, try to make both people feel affirmed.

5. Use touch whenever appropriate: Hold hands, link arms, give hugs, and use physical connection as effectively as you can.

6. Discover what brings the person joy: a time to talk, encouraging notes, a helping hand, or evening walks. Custom fit your attempts to bring joy.

7. Give them little surprises that will cause their eyes to light up, and let your eyes light up, too! The joy builds as the glances go back and forth.

8. Cherish babies and children by establishing through words and actions that you are authentically "glad to be with them."

cal or sexual abuse, many more suffer from the absences of good things that are necessary for emotional maturation, and *help is not usually available*. School failure, depression, anxiety, poor self-esteem, chronic physical illness, violent behavior, and disturbing sexual urges are some of the common after-effects of childhood traumas. When they go untreated, the children carry these effects along with them into adulthood. Woundedness, dividedness, isolation, and oppression are the result of leaving the trauma wounds unnoticed and unhealed. Too many people continue to suffer throughout their lives because they receive no attention for the effects of early abuse.

They really need for the people who love them to encourage them to find out where their pain is coming from, and to accompany them on their path to recovery. Without the help of a caring community around them, their woundedness, dividedness, isolation, and oppression will prevent them from getting to wholeness.

The Power of Joy

As we have seen, the world is a fracturing place, and each of us is split to some degree by the evil in the world. Yet within each of us is the drive to withstand the world's assaults, and to become the persons we were intended to be. God created us with minds that automatically seek to be whole, and the quest for wholeness is wonderfully boosted by joy during early childhood.

In a child's first two years, the desire to experience joy in loving relationships is the most powerful force in life. In fact, some neurologists now say that the basic human need is to be the "sparkle in someone's eye." When you catch a glimpse of a child's face as she runs toward an awaiting parent with arms outstretched in unrestrained joy, you can witness firsthand that incredible power that comes from "being the sparkle in someone's eye." When this joy is the strongest force in a child's world, life makes sense, because children look forward to moments when they can reconnect to joy – by being with their beloved. Wonderfully enough, that innocent, pure desire that begins in childhood continues throughout life. Life makes sense and is empowered by joy when people are in relationship with those who love them and are sincerely "glad to be with them."

Because joy is relational, it is also a contagious experience. Joy is produced when someone is "glad to see me", which stirs up a bit of joy in me. Then my joy is returned and the giver's joy is increased as well. This experience goes back-and-forth at amazingly fast rates – six cycles per second in a nonverbal, face-to-face exchange – all the time growing stronger "joy" between both people.

Joy also comes from being in a relationship with God. Throughout the Bible it is established that a powerful joy comes from a relationship with God who knows everything about me and is still "as-glad-as-glad-can-get" to be with me. Now, when ancient Biblical authors inspired by God, and 21st century neuroscientists propelled by knowledge all agree that joy comes through powerful relationships, we know there is something profoundly important to be learned from this.

In fact, when the joy strength is properly laid, just the knowledge that someone would be "glad to be with me," even if not physically present at the moment, is enough to return me to joy. Images of faces, the memory of their responses, and the presence of God can all sufficiently return us to joy.

When people get their joy properly connected to feelings that have been damaged by a fracturing world, they sense new power and aliveness in all of their relationships. The brain is designed to protect us from a damaging world, as we will see in Chapters 2 and 3, and it works very hard to repair the fractures. If functioning properly, the family and community are also designed to assist the brain in its jobs of protection and repair.

Particularly for those who are in recovery, it is essential to be in authentic, joy-producing relationships that can build joy strength and assist in returning to joy. If a person in recovery is not empowered by joy, it may be impossible to face the pain that is part of recovery. In fact, the amount of joy strength available needs to be higher than the amount of pain. Therefore, building joy through life-giving relationships is often the first part of recovery.

Having enough joy strength is fundamental to a person's well being. We now know that a "joy center" exists in the right orbital prefrontal cortex of the brain. It has executive control over the entire emotional system. When the joy center has been sufficiently developed, it regulates emotions, pain control and immunity centers; it guides us to act like ourselves; it releases neurotransmitters like dopamine and serotonin; and it is the only part of the brain that overrides the main drive centers – food and sexual impulses, terror and rage.

Recovery and Life

It takes a lifetime. Belonging to a family. Receiving and giving life. Overcoming the effects of traumas. Contributing to a community.

People do not get stuck when family and community smooth the pathway through these basics in life. Maturity progresses and God's redemption brings strength out of pain. If maturity stalls, *The Life Model* helps people find the stuck places. Therapy helps when it comes from authentic therapists, and if the clients' living environment supports it. This empowers people to live in bonds of love, so they can get unstuck on their way to wholeness.

The Life Model applies biblical truths to the human condition so that we can live in ways that will allow us to more fully experience God and His joy. Understanding *The Life Model* helps pinpoint what is going wrong, and suggests productive, realistic solutions – solutions that can last a lifetime, even though the process may not happen quickly.

A few therapeutic interventions have been discovered that can produce speedy "breakthroughs", and are at times presented as quick solutions for broken lives. Breakthroughs can be very important, but there is still the rest of life ahead. It is shortsighted to see a breakthrough as anything more than a small blip on the huge screen of life. *The Life Model* encompasses the whole screen. It is about much more than making therapy work better. It is about building up groups of people so they can have meaningful lives together; and it is about recovery for those who have been severely wounded, so that they can be woven into the fabric of their community and contribute from their hearts.

This book is an introduction to *The Life Model*. As you get further into the material, you will find the applications numerous: helping a whole community mature (see the *Maturity Indicators* chart in Chapter 2); finding someone's recovery needs (Chapter 3); creating life-giving families (Chapter 4); helping people live from their God-given identities (Chapter 5); and building a church where everyone profits because they live as the family of God (Chapter 6).

The Bible says the Kingdom of God is not about words, but about power (1 Corinthians 4:20). The ideas presented here are only as good as their results. If effective, *The Life Model* will give you a new appreciation for God's power that is available to you. It is intended to challenge you to live your life from the heart Jesus gave you, and that means life to the fullest. It will take your work and God's power, and it will take time. We, the therapists at

Shepherd's House, wish you God's best as you wade into this life-giving process!

If the material introduced so far is confusing or painful to you, please do not stop reading. As you continue to learn more about maturity, recovery, belonging, and the rest of *The Life Model*, we believe that everything will become clearer to you, and we hope that in the end, will bless both you and your community.

A Brief Summary

Life brings each of us inescapable traumas that block maturity. God's redemptive activity comes to us in two ways: He brings healing to our traumas, and adopts us into His family. Both ways boost us through our blocks to maturity, along the way to wholeness. With these boosts, we will be able to live from the hearts He gave us, our true identities will emerge, and our relationships with family and community will be characterized by joy.

Sometimes it is necessary to promote stronger relationships in a family and community before trauma recovery can proceed, and sometimes trauma recovery needs to take place before strong relationships can be established. Sometimes there needs to be more maturity before trauma recovery work can be effective, but other times we find that some trauma resolution needs to be achieved before maturity can get unstuck. There is no formula. When something is going wrong, assess maturity, trauma recovery, dividedness, family and community support, and spiritual vitality – and pray that the Lord will provide redemption wherever a deficit is found.

LESSON

2

WHOLENESS
Part 2

1. What does it mean to you to "seek God's redemption in the middle of the pain"? Pg 19-20
2. What has been your experience with the concept that redemption means that out of our greatest pain can come our most profound personal mission? Pg 19-20
3. Do you believe the past should be left in the past? Why or why not? If so, what do you think about the author's interpretation of Philippians 3? Pg 21-22
4. Define Type A trauma and explain what is needed to recover from it. Pg 21-22
5. Define Type B trauma and explain what is needed to recover from it. Pg 21-22
6. How does the Life Model define joy? In what ways is this the same and in what ways is it different from what you previously understood or were taught? Pg 26-28
7. What are the results/advantages of having a strongly developed joy center? Pg 26-28
8. How would your life and the lives in your church be different if you all were able to live from the hearts Jesus gave you, have your true identities emerge, and have relationships with family and community that were characterized by joy?

2

MATURITY

Maturity is about reaching one's God-given potential. It means maximizing our skills and talents, and using them effectively, while growing into the full capability of our individual designs.[1]

The information on maturity found in this chapter is the result of over 20 years of observation, research and experience. Jim Wilder was initially troubled by the fact that few people he encountered actually understood the fundamental tasks required to mature – and those who did understand usually could not produce words to teach it to others. Fortunately for us, he was inspired by

---

[1]   See *Living With Men* by Jim Wilder, for an expanded discussion of maturity.

the fact that important pockets of information from theology, psychology, medicine and neurology exist on the subject of maturity. So the study and synthesis began, and what you have before you is an introduction to those findings.

Chapter 1 introduced us to the idea that having sufficient joy strength lays the foundation for all other maturity and growth. Interestingly enough, a house with a faulty foundation can "look good" on the outside for several years, but eventually time, weather and stressful conditions will reveal the deficiency, and the house will begin the painful process of collapsing. Similarly, people without proper joy strength, which means an underdeveloped "joy center" in the right side of the brain, can appear "just fine" for the first 20 or sometimes even 30 years of life, but eventually life's wear and tear reveals the faulty construction, and the painful process of collapsing begins.

A house without a firm foundation, for example, cannot withstand the stress of a hailstorm or an earthquake, nor can it survive the pressure of remodeling. Similarly, a person without a firm joy foundation cannot withstand the stress of breakups or losses, nor survive the pressure of growth and maturity.

As you can see, laying foundations is vitally important work. Any architect knows that a good foundation contributes to the success and longevity of the entire building. So what happens then, you may ask, for those who did not get their joy foundation properly laid in the beginning? Are their chances for recovery and maturity completely destroyed?

Well, fortunately for us, during the last five years, neuroscience has made enormous strides in research, allowing us to answer this question. As we learn from emerging science and developmental research, we are always struck with God's infinite majesty and splendor. In His omnipotent wisdom God knew there would be deficiencies, so He created the brain with the capacity to compensate. While most of the brain stops growing at certain stages of development, the brain's "joy center", located in the right orbital prefrontal cortex, is the only section of the brain that never loses its capacity to grow! It is the one section of the brain that retains the ability to grow for our entire lives, which means that "joy strength" can always continue to develop!

What makes it grow, you may ask? It grows in response to real, joy-filled relationships. We are not talking about casual, superficial relationships here. But when people are engaged in authentic, bonded relationships showing real joy ("I'm delighted to be with you!"), this section of the brain will grow at any age! And while this brain growth is slower than during the optimum developmental periods, the bottom line is this – new foundations can be laid, damaged ones can be repaired, and stalled maturity does not have to remain impaired.

A Village and a Family*

Life in community is best when people have life-giving relationships with those in all the other stages of life. Infants need older children, adults, parents, and elders around them in order to learn the lessons that help each infant progress to life's next stage. The same is true for people in all the other stages. Elders need infants as much as infants need elders. We all need to have positive relationships with people in each of the other stages in order to achieve success in the stage of life we are in.

---

*   NOTE: The section on **Fear Bonds and Love Bonds** has been moved to the end of this chapter. The segment on **Replacing Fear Bonds With Love Bonds** has been changed to include maturity factors. The original version of **Fear Bonds and Love Bonds** can now be found in Appendix A.

Maturity never ends, and people need ongoing family and community relationships to stay unstuck in maturity. People need to know who they are, and they need to be frequently reminded of who they are by those who love them. As we will see in Chapter 4, belonging to a family is for everyone, especially for widows, orphans, those without children, and single people.

The 1996 American presidential campaign entertained a heated debate between Republicans and Democrats, arguing whether it takes a family or a village to best raise a child. We are here to say, after carefully studying the conditions that affect human maturity, that we are convinced beyond a doubt it takes *both* a village and a family to most successfully raise a child.

Maturity Stages

Here is an overview of the maturity stages. A person's physical age does not determine his or her maturity level, but the satisfactory completion of the maturity requirements does. Each stage includes all the needs and tasks of the previous ones. The ages listed indicate when the tasks can first be achieved. They cannot be achieved ahead of time, but they can be made up later in life if there are deficiencies. "The Maturity Indicators" explanations and the chart at the end of this chapter will clarify this information more fully.

Infant (0 - 3). Throughout this discussion we use the term "infant" broadly to include both children and adults, in the 0 – 3 year old stage of development.

The infant's fundamental need is to *receive* unconditional love and care. Receiving always precedes giving. We will never be able to effectively give until we have received. When our fundamental dependency needs have been met, we are motivated to become independent and start caring for ourselves. *If our primary dependency needs are not met, we will spend the rest of our lives trying to get others to take care of us.* Therefore for most of this stage, parents need to supply the infant's needs by recognizing when the young person needs to be fed or hugged or comforted or rocked to sleep. Training and discipline are necessary as the baby enters toddlerhood, of course, but good training does not undermine the overriding need for the 0 – 3 child to learn to *receive.*

As already stated, joy development is the foundation of this first stage. Infants need to be the "sparkle in someone's eye" and to be with people that are "glad to be with them" so that they live in joy and learn that joy is one's normal state. These conditions actually grow the "joy center" of the brain that will have "executive control" over their emotional systems for the rest of their lives. While most of the first year of development is committed to building joy, the child over 12 months begins the important task of returning to joy from every unpleasant emotion.

Some infants are "high need" babies and need parents who respond to their signs of desperation by delivering as much life as is needed. While ignoring baby's cries in an attempt to control the crying may get them to stop crying, this approach does not provide the safety or comfort that are vital to their future adult development.

Developing trust through bonding with parents is also crucial during this stage. This bonding requires time, touch and togetherness with both parents invested and involved. Infants also begin the process of developing pictures of who they are in this stage, based on images of other significant faces looking at them. When an infant is surrounded by others who see her in the same way God sees her, the person she was designed to be, these faces will communicate to her at a very young age her value and importance.

"Adult infants" who have not received in these important areas as babies, will always be needy as adults. They will not be able to take care of themselves emotionally nor will they be able to appropriately receive important things from others. Adult infants will not ask for what they need because they believe if others really cared for them, they would figure out what they needed. Adult infants cannot handle criticism even if it is valid and constructive, because they see any negative feedback as a personal attack. They are often possessive of relationships, territory, power and possessions. Unfortunately for all involved, they also use fear bonding to ensure others will stay bonded to them. And while "high functioning" adult infants can appear responsible in many areas, like handling personal finances, and being punctual and reliable, emotionally they are severely crippled making it very difficult for them to have successful and enduring relationships.

Child (4 - 12). When the infant learns to say what is needed, that marks a transition to the next stage. It is cause for celebration when a child can leave babyhood behind and begin learning to care for self. As the child moves toward puberty, it is still important to receive love without earning it. Rewards are to be earned, but not love – it is to be unconditional. Whenever a child is required to take care of a parent, things are backwards. Although "parentified" children who have to physically or emotionally take care of adults can appear mature on the outside, their needs are not being sufficiently filled and this will at some time impair their emotional development, leaving deficiencies.

Learning to care for oneself requires the mastering of several personal tasks. (1) A child must learn to say what he thinks and feels and appropriately ask for what is needed. When adults have not learned how to do this they often are frustrated because their needs do not get met and their voices do not get heard. (2) Children must learn what brings them satisfaction. If people never learn what satisfies, others will determine what is satisfying for them. (3) Children need to learn how to do hard things. This requires developing patience and persistence, and takes some guidance. Unfortunately for all, there is a current "entitlement" trend in America. It erroneously suggests that if you are worthwhile, you will not have to do hard things. This misconception goes against all conventional wisdom and severely limits the development of maturity. (4) Children need to develop their personal talents and resources. Otherwise, they are highly susceptible to filling their lives with unsatisfying and unproductive activities. (5) Self care requires knowing yourself and making yourself understandable to others. (6) Children need to understand how they fit into history as well as the "big picture" of life. By studying their personal histories, children can understand the present better and be more effective in molding the future. When children understand the "big picture" of life, they realize that they have the ability to personally impact the world.

"Child adults" who have adult bodies but are emotionally at the child level of maturity, will always appear egocentric. Unlike "infant adults" who cannot take care of themselves, "child adults" can take care of themselves but they can *only* take care of themselves – and often that is at the expense of others.

Adult (13 - birth of first child). You will know when a person has graduated from the child level of maturity to the adult level because he will shift from being a self-centered child to a both-centered adult. While a child needs to learn me-centered fairness (how do I make it fair for me), an adult learns we-centered fairness (how do I make it fair for us). Mutuality is the trademark of an adult because he can take care of two people at the same time. When people with adult bodies are functioning below the adult level of maturity, you will know because in the end your interactions with them will never feel mutual. You will go away feeling like in order to maintain a relationship with them you will always need to give more, listen more or tolerate more than they would ever be willing to do for you.

Adults know how to remain stable in difficult situations and can return self and others to joy. People who cannot do this will either avoid, escape or get stuck in certain emotions, crippling many of their endeavors and relationships. For example, if I avoid all anger, it eventually explodes into rage. If I get stuck in shame and failure, I may become depressed or even suicidal. And if I escape pain and rejection by doing drugs or having a sordid affair, I've only increased my misery and suffering.

Bonding with peers and developing a group identity are also important adult tasks. Young adults thrive when they are allowed to use appropriate power, gain success in peer relationships, and seek truth and fairness for their society.

Having the opportunity to effectively contribute to and be a part of a vital community are also necessary. Being part of something bigger than "me" is both empowering and inspiring.

Lastly, an adult needs to express the characteristics of her heart in a deepening personal way. Once people know who they truly are and understand the power and beauty of their God-given characteristics, their passion, purpose, talents, and pain will all come together and begin to define specifically who they are. The better they can express their unique identities in their words and actions, the more positioned they will be for speaking and living truthfully.

Parent (*first birth until youngest child becomes an adult*). Biologically being a parent does not automatically put you at the parent stage of maturity. In fact, many parents are not at this level. You know that you are at the parent stage, however, when you can sacrificially care for your children without resenting the sacrifice or expecting to receive anything for your efforts. You may feel exhausted or overwhelmed at times, but you still will be able to appreciate, not begrudge, your sacrifice. Unfortunately, an "entitlement" philosophy also pervades modern parenting. "I'm entitled to do all the things I was doing as an adult, and I should not have to make any sacrifices of time, money or social activities." We want to be clear here. Parenting does involve sacrifice, but it is not about giving up who you are. It is about becoming who you are!

It is vitally important for parents to learn how to protect, serve and enjoy their families. When a parent is doing all three, everyone in the family will be fulfilled. Balancing these three requires support from the community and guidance from mature parents who have already paved the way.

Mature parents are also aware that they alone cannot provide everything their children will need. Therefore, these parents are wise in allowing and providing spiritual family members – other important people in their children's lives who will help their children become the persons they were designed to be.

Additionally, mature parents will be able to bring their children through difficult times and return to joy from all unpleasant emotions. As you can see, the ability to return to joy is forever important.

In the end, mature parenting is about representing God to one's family. When you accomplish that, you are ready to graduate to the final level of maturity.

Elder (beginning when youngest child becomes an adult). Sadly, most in our culture never make it to this level of maturity. This is unfortunate because the success of any country, community, school or church body will have a direct correlation to the presence of true elders who are guiding and advising. To qualify as an elder, one needs to have raised children to maturity and completed all the prior maturity tasks.

True elders can act like themselves in the midst of difficulty. They can also establish an accurate community identity by *finding out* what their community has been designed by God to be, rather than imposing what they would like it to be. Furthermore, true elders prize all community members and see them as God sees them – looking past their flaws and facades to see the persons they have been designed to be.

True elders are also willing and able to parent and mature the community. They are qualified to do this because they have learned from a lifetime of experiences. They can handle criticism and rejection, speak the truth even when it is not easy or popular, serve without being appreciated, encourage needed growth and change, delight in younger people's skill and power, and place what is best for the community over personal fairness or preference.

Lastly, true elders realize that those without sufficient biological families need real, live, loving spiritual families to heal, to grow and to thrive. Therefore, true elders are open to God's voice when He orchestrates a spiritual adoption, and are willing to give spiritual children the same unselfish care that they gave their own biological children.

Making the Transition Between Stages

It is helpful for maturing people to understand that when the beginning of each new maturity stage approaches, anxiety increases substantially. For example, it is tough entering puberty (junior high school is loaded with anxiety) and it is also anxiety producing to enter any of the other stages, like launching the final offspring and becoming a *true* elder in the community. When the community knows that anxiety will undoubtedly accompany passages into the next stage, it helps people get through transitions. If such a naturally occurring problem is called something like "mid-life crisis," however, that does not provide much help with the anxiety. *But knowing that anxiety is a normal part of passing between maturity stages allows a whole new energy that actually propels the transition process.* With this fresh, needed energy, the problem can be identified – certain tasks from earlier stages may not be completed yet, which can certainly be anxiety producing. But the excitement of the growth coupled with the guidance from others who are more mature will allow the person to persevere through this anxiety barrier, and make it to the next stage. You can see why people need an entire community to get through life's transitions.

Maturity never finishes, and people never stop needing other people. They do best when they live in groups of families, made up of individuals who help each other get unstuck in the areas that block their progress. They know who they are, live from their hearts, and see each other as God sees them.

It is clear that there are lessons to be learned during each stage. Reaching the physical age where the next stage is supposed to begin guarantees *only* that the body will be ready; it guarantees nothing about the actual maturity level. When the body is ahead of the overall maturity level, problems can develop. Perhaps the most popular prototypic example of such a lag in maturity is seen in comics. A grown man is shown making childish mistakes, and we are supposed to laugh. And while it is comical to laugh at men who are depicted as children running around in grown bodies, it is not fun to be married to one. Many men are not given good training during infancy to learn to say clearly what they need or how they feel, and they may not know much about meeting the needs of others. That is not a joke – it is a problem that begs to be solved. It is good to begin finding the solution by correctly identifying the problem – unfinished maturity tasks. When they have identified the uncompleted tasks or needs, it is important to know that people can catch up. But, there is more to learn about maturity before we take a look at catching up.

The Growth, Brokenness and Transformation Cycle

A pattern in maturity is essential in building a person's identity. It happens at transition points between life's stages, but it can also happen during growth periods. When it recurs, people understand themselves and others better, and therefore are better prepared to love. That is where the transformation cycle is supposed to lead. While growth is underway, tension builds over time, coming to a head, and there is a point where brokenness takes place. Without fear, the cycle leads to a transformation and a fresh appreciation of life. Perhaps an example from Jim Friesen's life would illustrate how this looks.

During the first two years he spent learning how to be therapeutic with people who dissociate, Jim found himself working very hard and growing, but sensing he was spinning his wheels. He had read that dissociative clients who stay in treatment tend to get better, but that was becoming more doubtful as he went along. A few did not stay in treatment, and some were getting much worse instead of better. He began to wonder if the therapeutic approach he was learning was correct. Eventually, he despairingly concluded that the material he was working so hard to learn was not actually helping people.

Anxiety was building. He had spent about twelve years striving to build an identity as a psychologist – getting the degrees, going through the licensing process, investing thousands of hours developing clinical skills, and then plunging into a specialty area, only to find that clinical psychology did not produce the expected results. Anxiety was appropriate to the circumstances. Brokenness was setting in, accompanied by despair and hopelessness.

Recognizing he could not help these people using only psychological interventions, he decided to get training in how to use spiritual interventions along with the psychological principles he had already learned. The next two years found him being broken and transformed into a Christian who is a psychologist instead of a psychologist who is a Christian. He passed from the child stage of maturity, in becoming a therapist, to an adult. No longer was it enough for him to stick, in a child-like fashion, to "tried and true" therapy methods. His identity was turned into something completely new during this training – he gained confidence in the spiritual material, and was transformed into an adult who could understand people better and give them what their hearts needed – psychological and spiritual interventions that worked together. That was the cycle. The clients got unstuck, and so did he!

The transformation cycle can take place periodically throughout life, and is often accompanied by anxiety, depression or other new feelings. Transformations can follow healing or can take place during the completion of a normal maturity stage. Transformation gives a person a new identity when the old one is broken or too small. The pain can be very intense, but that is always part of the cycle that leads to wholeness. As the cycle is completed, a more fully developed self emerges, life skills increase, and so does joy.

Maturity demands that people honestly face their traumas, even when it is quite painful. Transformation is not achieved any other way. The core experience of therapy is trauma recovery – allowing God to repair the brokenness, becoming transformed, and moving on to more growth. What therapy has to offer is to assist people in respectfully repairing their brokenness. Identity expands when the transformation cycle is completed, leading to higher levels of maturity.

LESSON

3

MATURITY
Part 1

1. What is your response to the Life Model's definition of maturity? How is this view the same and how is it different from your previous understanding?   Pg 33
2. What signs or events might indicate that a person's life is collapsing as a result of an inadequate joy foundation?   Pg 34
3. An infant's primary need is to receive, and if this need is not met, "we spend the rest of our lives trying to get others to take care of us." What does this look like in adults who did not learn how to receive?   Pg 36-38
4. What have you observed with "high functioning" "adult infants" who are responsible in many areas, but have difficultly in having successful and enduring relationships?   Pg 38
5. What are some examples of the behaviors of "child adults" who can only take care of themselves, often at the expense of others?   Pg 38-39
6. People with parent level maturity can sacrificially care for their children without resenting the sacrifice or expecting to receive anything for their efforts. What are some examples of what this would look like?   How is this different from martyrs who "give up everything" for their children?   Pg 41
7. Asking people who are above us in maturity to help identify the maturity tasks that we have not yet completed can propel us to our next level.   Who can you ask to help you with this? Pg 43-44

How People Mature

We are ready to see how these three *Life Model* components work together: maturity, recovery, and belonging. They cannot be understood apart from one another. People have a God-given, inner desire to increase their maturity so they will be able to live from their hearts. Maturity is often blocked, however, and the blocks usually come from absences in the other two areas – from unfinished trauma recovery, and from the lack of life-giving relationships.

On page 53 you will find a table entitled "*Maturity Indicators.*" That table includes three columns: "Personal Tasks" is on the left, "Community and Family Tasks" in the middle, and "When the Tasks Fail" on the right. Maturation *requires two elements*: (1) The individual completes the maturity tasks (the first column), and (2) the family and community provide whatever is necessary for maturation (the middle column). Failure to complete these tasks is quite serious, and leads to the failures listed in the third column.

Please take a detailed look at how each task in one column relates to the other tasks in the same row. This chart illustrates quite dramatically just how interdependent people are in the maturation process. When family and community fail, a deficit will show up in the middle column, and a "Type A" trauma (the absence of something necessary for growth) is the direct result. The maturing individual will not be able to complete all the personal tasks (the left column), and a problem will show up as a failure in the right column.

The *Maturity Indicators* chart clarifies how trauma recovery is related to maturity, and how it is dependent on particular kinds of input from family and community. Persons cannot become prepared to give life unless they first receive it. The middle column represents maturity training, and the left column is where it is accomplished. As people progress through each stage, they become equipped to help others complete those same tasks. In cases where family and community fail to meet the needs of younger people, the youth are likely to be inadequately prepared, and the deficits that show up in the right column can become life-draining to their families and communities.

Will people grow up to be life-giving or life-draining? The family and community are the people who create the environment that nudges offspring in one of those two directions. One of those directions is guided by love bonds; the other is guided by fear bonds. That preparation for becoming a person, life-giving or life-draining, is then passed on to the next generation. We are all trained in this way to give others life – or to drain it from them.

But do not think that nothing can be done to correct faulty training. People create history – they become an active part of their world. The word "create" packs a lot of meaning. People can overcome shortcomings that result from faulty training, they can receive repair for traumas, and that can introduce improvements into the lives of those who are still in training. That is good news. People can help one another get unstuck and begin to mature once again. No wonder the Bible is so emphatic about loving one another, bearing each other's burdens, and being an active participant in the family of God!

The Maturity Indicators Chart

As you look at the third column of *Maturity Indicators*, do not be surprised if you find that the effects of stalled maturity are very widespread. The therapists at Shepherd's House have found that when people come for help, many times there are uncompleted maturity tasks which limit the client's ability to receive and give life. Our extensive study of maturity has taught us several important lessons. Here are eight of those lessons that need to be highlighted so that you will be ready to study the *Maturity Indicators* chart.

All people desire maturity but few know how to attain it or to teach it to others. Ask yourself if you know how to increase your maturity or to help others increase theirs. If you do not, you are not alone. Most people we talk to do not have language or guidelines for maturity. That is why we feel passionate about including maturity in *The Life Model*.

As a whole, our American culture does poorly in the area of maturation, and, sadly enough, the majority of our population probably operates at the infant or child level of maturity. This reality becomes evident when you look at our broken marriages, abused and neglected children, high levels of violence, and substance abuse and sexual addiction problems. This reality is another powerful reason for us to teach people about maturity.

Maturity is not a spiritual gift nor is it a byproduct of salvation. It is something we, as Christians, must work at our whole lives. Salvation, deliverance, healing and redemption – these are all God's domain. God graciously and miraculously does all these things for us because we cannot do them for ourselves. But maturity is our domain. James 1:4 instructs us to become mature and complete, not lacking anything. This reference is one of many portions of Scripture that highlight our responsibility to work on maturity. At the end of this manuscript there is a page, entitled "Biblical Underpinnings For The Life Model," with a list of other passages that stress the importance of maturity.

Raising maturity levels increases the success and satisfaction of marriages, parenting and leadership. As Christians it becomes both dangerous and non-Biblical to rest on our laurels and arrogantly assume that because we are saved, we are automatically mature. This erroneous belief is exactly what keeps non-Christians skeptical of Christians. They ask, "Why would I want to become a Christian?

My non-Christian friends treat me better (more maturely) than my Christian friends." Christians can become disillusioned because of this erroneous belief as well, declaring, "I cannot believe that Christians treated me so immaturely!" Not only does evangelism suffer, but without higher levels of maturity, Christians will struggle in their marriages, ministries, and parenting. Christians are called to become mature and they need to continually work at it – both for their own lives and in order for their churches to experience the richness that a maturing community brings.

A person's physical age or stage does not determine his or her maturity level. The *Maturity Indicators* age ranges listed for each stage indicate the periods of time during which the listed tasks can *first* be achieved. If they are achieved during later stages, that is certainly still good.

Each stage includes all the needs and tasks of previous stages. Maturity is a building-upon-previous-lessons experience. If you have had an algebra class, you know what this means. In order for you to learn each new lesson you have to retain the previous lessons, or the new lesson will not be understood. Maturity requires that the tasks are to be accomplished in successive stages, or people will get stuck right where they are.

A lack of "family" and unresolved pain from traumas can severely block the process of maturity. Chapters 3 and 4 discuss removing those blocks.

Maturity does *not* increase or determine a person's value. *You are still valuable whatever your maturity stage may be.*

Have the Courage to Pursue Maturity

Please understand, as you study this chart, that it will be most useful to you *if you have the courage to be honest about any shortfalls in your own maturity.* The purpose of this chart is not to prove how mature we are — the purpose of the chart is to identify our weak areas so we can work on them and *become more mature*. The chart is not a complete listing of all stage-related tasks, but it underlines certain key areas of work for each stage of development.[2]

Pray for *wisdom* to personally discern the ways in which your own maturity may be impaired, and the ways in which you could provide more nurturing and growth for those around you who are needing to mature. It would also be helpful to get feedback about your maturity from people who know and love you. They can be important mirrors to help you see yourself better.

You will find shortfalls in your maturity, but through God's power, and through God-ordained relationships, maturity can be attained. Communities work as they should when individuals contribute to each other — when they receive life and give it. "Being mature" is part individual, part family, and part community. If there is a shortfall in maturity, people can catch up, through their own willingness, with help from others, and by the power of God.

You can create a better life for yourself and for others. Examine the *Maturity Indicators* and then think about your fears. Perhaps they protect you from frightening feelings that come from B traumas and keep you stuck at the child-level, blocking your confidence to "do hard things." Or your depression may stem from an A trauma, like not belonging, which keeps you isolated. Immaturity may stifle the characteristics of your heart. As you work toward maturity, however, the true characteristics of your heart will become more evident to you and to those around you. As stated earlier, progress in maturity increases success in marriage, parenting and leadership. Friendships become deeper, and relationships become more mutually satisfying. Gains in maturity help you live from the heart Jesus gave you, in a more deeply satisfying way.

---

[2]   For a more inclusive listing, see Jim Wilder's *Living With Men*.

The Life Model: **MATURITY INDICATORS**

THE INFANT STAGE: BIRTH THROUGH AGE 3

Newborns and toddlers are included here, up to the age where they can effectively say what their needs are.

PRIMARY TASK to be completed during this stage:
Learning to receive.

PRIMARY RESULTING PROBLEM in adult life when tasks are not completed:
Weak or stormy relationships.

	PERSONAL TASKS	COMMUNITY AND FAMILY TASKS	WHEN THE TASKS FAIL
1.	Lives in joy: Expands capacity for joy, learns that joy is one's normal state, and builds joy strength.	Parents delight in the infant's wonderful and unique existence.	Weak identity; fear and coldness dominate bonds with others.
2.	Develops trust.	Parents build strong, loving, bonds with the infant – bonds of unconditional love.	Has difficulty bonding – which often leads to manipulative, self-centered, isolated, or discontented personality.
3.	Learns how to receive.	Gives care that matches the infant's needs, without the infant asking.	Is withdrawn, disengaged, self-stimulating, and unresponsive.
4.	Begins to organize self into a person through relationships.	Discovers the true characteristics of the infant's unique identity, through attention to the child's behavior and character.	Has an inability to regulate emotions.
5.	Learns how to return to joy from every unpleasant emotion.	Provides enough safety and companionship during difficulties, so the infant can return to joy from any other emotion.	Has uncontrollable emotional outbursts, excessive worry and depression. Avoids, escapes or gets stuck in certain emotions.

The Life Model: **MATURITY INDICATORS**

THE CHILD STAGE: AGE 4 THROUGH 12

Age 12 is the earliest age this stage can be completed.

PRIMARY TASK to be completed during this stage:
Taking care of self.

PRIMARY RESULTING PROBLEM in adult life when tasks are not completed:
Not taking responsibility for self.

	PERSONAL TASKS	COMMUNITY AND FAMILY TASKS	WHEN THE TASKS FAIL
1.	Asks for what is needed – can say what one thinks and feels.	Teaches and allows child to appropriately articulate needs.	Experiences continual frustration and disappointment because needs are not met; is often passive-aggressive.
2.	Learns what brings personal satisfaction.	Helps child to evaluate the consequences of own behaviors, and to identify what satisfies him or her.	Is obsessed with or addicted to food, drugs, sex, money, or power, in a desperate chase to find satisfaction.
3.	Develops enough persistence to do hard things.	Challenges and encourages child to do difficult tasks the child does not feel like doing.	Experiences failure, remains stuck and undependable, is consumed with comfort and fantasy life.
4.	Develops personal resources and talents.	Provides opportunities to develop the child's unique talents and interests.	Fills life with unproductive activities, despite God-given abilities.
5.	Knows self and takes responsibility to make self understandable to others.	Guides in discovering the unique characteristics of the child's heart.	Fails to develop true identity; conforms to outside influences that misshape identity.
6.	Understands how he or she fits into history as well as the "big picture" of what life is about.	Educates the child about the family history as well as the history of the family of God.	Feels disconnected from history and is unable to protect self from family lies or dysfunctions that are passed on.

The Life Model: **MATURITY INDICATORS**

THE ADULT STAGE: AGE 13 TO BIRTH OF 1st CHILD

Age 13 is the earliest age at which adult-level tasks may be accomplished.

PRIMARY TASK to be completed during this stage:
Taking care of two people simultaneously.

PRIMARY RESULTING PROBLEM when this task is not completed:
Lacks the capacity to be in mutually satisfying relationships.

	PERSONAL TASKS	COMMUNITY AND FAMILY TASKS	WHEN THE TASKS FAIL
1.	Cares for self and others simultaneously in mutually satisfying relationships.	Provides the opportunity to participate in group life.	Is self-centered, leaves other people dissatisfied and frustrated.
2.	Remains stable in difficult situations, and knows how to return self and others to joy.	Affirms that the young adult will make it through difficult times.	Conforms to peer pressure, and participates in negative and destructive group activities.
3.	Bonds with peers; develops group identity.	Provides positive environment and activities where peers can bond.	Is a loner, with tendencies to isolate; shows excessive self-importance.
4.	Takes responsibility for how personal actions affect others, including protecting others from self.	Teaches young adults that their behaviors impact others and impact history.	Is controlling, harmful, blaming, and unprotective to others.
5.	Contributes to the community; articulates "who we are", as part of belonging to the community.	Provides opportunities to be involved in important community tasks.	Does not become a life-giving contributor to the community, is self-absorbed and uses others – drains society.
6.	Expresses the characteristics of his or her heart in a deepening personal style.	Holds the person accountable, while still accepting and affirming the aspects of his or her true self.	Is driven to "play roles", prove self to the world, get results, and seek approval.

The Life Model: **MATURITY INDICATORS**

THE PARENT STAGE:
BIRTH OF 1st CHILD UNTIL YOUNGEST CHILD IS AN ADULT

PRIMARY TASK to be completed during this stage:
Sacrificially taking care of children.

PRIMARY RESULTING PROBLEM when tasks are not accomplished:
Distant or conflicted family relationships

	PERSONAL TASKS	COMMUNITY AND FAMILY TASKS	WHEN THE TASKS FAIL
1.	Protects, serves, and enjoys one's family.	The community gives the opportunity for both parents to sacrificially contribute to their family.	Family members are (1) at risk, (2) deprived, and (3) feel worthless or unimportant.
2.	Is devoted to taking care of children without expecting to be taken care of by the children in return.	The community promotes devoted parenting.	Children have to take care of parents, which is impossible, and often leads to (1) child abuse/neglect and/or (2) "parentified" children – which actually blocks their maturity instead of facilitating it.
3.	Allows and provides spiritual parents and siblings for their children.	The community encourages relationships between children and extended spiritual family members.	Children are vulnerable to peer pressure, to cults, to any misfortune, and are less likely to succeed in life's goals. Parents get overwhelmed without extended family support.
4.	Learns how to bring children through difficult times, and return to joy from other emotions.	The community supports parents by giving them encouragement, guidance, breaks, and opportunities to recharge.	Hopeless, depressed, disintegrating family units develop.

The Life Model: **MATURITY INDICATORS**

THE ELDER STAGE:
BEGINNING WHEN YOUNGEST CHILD HAS BECOME AN ADULT

PRIMARY TASK to be completed during this stage:
Sacrificially taking care of the community

PRIMARY RESULTING PROBLEM when this task is not accomplished:
The overall maturity of the community declines.

	PERSONAL TASKS	COMMUNITY AND FAMILY TASKS	WHEN THE TASKS FAIL
1.	Establishes an accurate community identity, and acts like self in the midst of difficulty.	The community recognizes elders in the community.	There is meaninglessness, disorder, loss of direction, and disintegration of all social structures from government to family.
2.	Prizes each community member, and enjoys the true self in each individual.	The community provides opportunities for elders to be involved with those in all of the other maturity stages.	Life-giving interactions diminish, along with life-giving interdependence, stunting the community's growth. Fragile, at-risk people fail to heal or survive.
3.	Parents and matures the community.	The community creates a structure to help the elders do their job, which allows people at every stage of maturity to interact properly with those in other stages, and listen to the wisdom of maturity.	When elders do not lead, unqualified people do, resulting in immature interactions at every level of the community.
4.	Gives life to those without a family through spiritual adoption.	Places a high value on being a spiritual family to those with no family.	When the "familyless" are not individually taken care of, poverty, violence, crisis, crime, and mental disorders increase.

LESSON

4

MATURITY
Part 2

1. What are the two things that block our God-given inner desire to become mature? Explain what these mean to you. Pg 48
2. Describe your understanding of the ongoing cycle of receiving and giving life that occurs between the individual and the community that is necessary for growth and maturity to develop appropriately? Pg 48-49
3. Do you agree with the statement that "…the majority of our population probably operates at the infant or the child level of maturity"? Why or why not? Pg 50-51
4. What has been your experience with the impact of immature Christians on the reputation of Jesus and the church? Pg 50
5. What is your understanding of why maturity requires that the tasks must be accomplished in successive stages and that they build upon each other in sequence? Pg 51
6. Read through each maturity stage in the Maturity Indicators Chart and mark the personal tasks that you have mastered. Based on your age and the skills you have developed, what would you say would best describe you maturity level at this point? What do you think about this? Pg 53-57
7. How does it impact you to know that you are valuable no matter what your current maturity level? Pg 51.

* An optional free Maturity Skills Assessment is available at
joystartshere.com.

Fear Bonds and Love Bonds*

Becoming mature requires bonds between people – they are the foundation upon which maturity is built. Bonds are the connections that energize us, motivate our actions and establish our identities. The receiving-and-giving exchange in our bonds shapes our view of what really is important. There are two essentially different and incompatible types of bonds – one based on fear and the other on love. Fear bonds are formed around avoiding negative feelings and pain. Love bonds are formed around desire, joy and seeking to be with people who are important to us. Fear bonds energize people to avoid pain – like rejection, fear, shame, humiliation, abandonment, guilt or even physical abuse. Love bonds motivate people to live in truth, closeness, joy, peace, perseverance, kindness and authentic giving. (See the chart on page 69.)

When people share a bond of love, a special kind of energy flows between them. As their eyes connect, there is a sparkle that energizes them both. They look forward to being together because they desire the special closeness they share. When the shared bond is governed by fear, anxiety builds as the time approaches to be together. Fear can also develop from being apart.

The fear bonds and love bonds we experience during formative years determine the way we motivate ourselves. When fearful, we threaten ourselves with what will happen if we do not get to work on time, lose weight, save money, or keep our partner from getting mad. We think about things that could go wrong. We worry, feel guilty, run from shame, and blame others. We become emotionally paralyzed. We operate way *under* our potential.

---

* NOTE: This section on **Fear Bonds and Love Bonds** was moved here from the beginning of the chapter for this study guide revision.

Love bonds, on the other hand, motivate us to remain faithful under pressure, to help others to be all they were created to be, to be willing to endure pain in order to be close to those we love, and to tell the truth even when it hurts. We think about how God sees others. We are not controlled by fear because we know there is always something more important that demands our attention and devotion. There is no fear in love because perfect love casts out fear.

Fear bonds and love bonds can exist together in the same family or individual. Ultimately one fear bond or love bond will become the most influential. That fear or love bond will increase until it dominates the person, or it may even dominate the whole family. As we grow, heal and mature we leave behind fear bonds and replace them with love bonds. We are guided by goals we desire, rather than by avoiding the disasters we fear. The only fear that ultimately makes sense is to fear God because if we keep our eyes on God out of fear, we will always discover that He loves us.

Changing Motivation From Fear to Love*

Our direction and goals come from our thoughts. Our motivation comes from our emotions. While we work very hard to educate our thoughts and correct our beliefs, few people train or perfect their motivation with equal discipline. As far as our nervous systems are concerned, our minds run well when motivated by love and desire, and poorly when motivated by fear. From a moral point of view, love is also superior. Perfect, mature love (teleios in the Greek) casts out fear. (1 John 4:18)

---

* NOTE: This section on changing motivation from fear to love was not written by the original authors and was added here by the editors of this edition. The original text can be found in Appendix A This replacement text written in 2004 by Jim Wilder includes a more complete discussion of maturity as a factor.

Fear motives creep into our lives when we fail to mature properly. We form our motivation during infancy through bonded relationships. Whatever emotions our parents use to motivate us become our internal source of motivation as well. If our early bonds form from love they serve us well but if bonds form from fear and the avoidance of pain, our motivational system stays immature.

Fear-bonds form as the result of failed attempts at self-preservation. We do need fear as one of our emotions because it motivates self-preservation. However, when fear dominates early relationships and we feel we cannot escape, fear becomes our main guidance system. We begin to avoid pain as a form of self-preservation. Once avoiding pain becomes our focus, we avoid pain even when there is no real risk of overwhelming our capacity.

Once we are fear-bonded and motivated to avoid pain we think and say things like:

"What if he gets mad?"

"Are you going to be upset?"

"I'm afraid that..."

"I'd be too embarrassed!"

"You are really making me mad!"

"I have to make him/it stop."

"I can't stand it when..."

"What difference will it make?"

We must then ask this serious question about avoiding pain. *Is it self-preservation if I stop being and acting like myself?* When I no longer speak or act like who I am inside isn't my "self" lost? When I can no longer even figure out what I want, feel or even think, haven't I lost my "self" already?

We are afraid to make an impact on others. We become confused about what fears are our fears and which ones belong to others. Being around anxious people makes us edgy. We withdraw, placate, entertain or please others. We take on responsibilities that are not ours because we are afraid of what will happen if we don't. We feel inadequate. Thinking we are preserving ourselves, we have lost our souls.

We also fear allowing others to be in control because we fear losing our own impact. We control people around us with anger, contempt, rejection, ridicule, physical violence, the "silent treatment" and other ways of creating pain. We have lost our flavor. We are no longer lights in the world.

Before we can understand how to change a fear-bond back to a love-bond, let us consider how a healthy identity would deal with fears at each level of development.

Avoiding Fear-Bonds at Each Level of Maturity

1. Infant maturity
   a. Recognize the fear (what am I really afraid of?)
   b. Know who I want with me when I am afraid
   c. Discover what I want (desire)
   d. Talk about my fear

2. Child Maturity
   a. Recognize my part in the fearful situation
   b. Recognize the other person's part in the fearful situation
   c. Use a third person to check my reality
   d. Separate my responsibility from yours (a+b)
   e. Learn to be myself rather than control others

3. Adult
   a. Stay in relationship while letting others have fears
   b. Do nothing about what others fear-let them handle it
   c. Take care of our own business with personal style
   d. Remind self and others about our mutual goals and desires

There is a big separation between adult and higher levels of maturity when it comes to handling fears. Up to this point every person is responsible for their own fears and no one else's. Without many years of practice distinguishing this fear is mine from that fear is yours, moving to higher levels of dealing with fear will only bring confusion about responsibility. The shift of responsibility from dealing with my own fears to helping others with their fears is a major sign of dysfunction when it is attempted by anyone of adult maturity or lower. Even for parents, taking on the fears of others is dysfunctional outside the parent/child relationship.

Parents must be very careful not to develop fear-bonds in their children. Since parents want to build capacity in their children, they help children back to joy from fear and teach them to act like themselves during manageable levels of the emotion.

4. Parent
   a. Help one's personal people (natural and spiritual family)
   b. Take some shared responsibility for the fears of younger minds
   c. Identify fears in younger mind
   d. Help younger mind return to joy and peace
5. Elder
   a. Help "at risk," isolated, marginalized people
   b. Identify community fears
   c. Help community remember what is like us to do
   d. Remain a non-anxious presence

Elders, as we know, act like parents-at-large for their communities. Elders will provide just barely enough security for people to recognize and face their own fears, knowing that they are not alone and remembering what is really important to "our people" under these scary conditions.

Converting Fear to Love Based on Our Maturity Level

To make a change from fear to love, we start first with the adult level. If we can correct the problem at this level it will be easiest. The adult simply thinks and decides differently.

1. Confidently be ourselves. Take care of our business. Stay in relationship with others around us who are anxious, but do nothing about their part of the problem. Speak of mutual goals that are important during this time of threat and fear.

If this adult solution worked, then we have corrected the fear bond. This does not mean that others will not react by trying to put pressure on us to become frightened again, so we may have to make this correction several times under even more pressure and anxiety from others.

If you still feel fear or cannot imagine how to use an adult solution, we must go deeper and correct some earlier problems that lead to fear bonds. First we look at the child level skills. Resolving fear-bonds at the child level is not just a matter of understanding and choosing differently. These solutions take longer and involve study and consultation with others. They require a good deal of problem solving to figure out "mine" from "yours." We do not solve these problems without consultation and encouragement.

2. Define your responsibilities carefully. Go through the demands you feel and see which ones are logically yours and which are unreasonable. Find someone qualified to double-check your judgment. Next, be clear when you are trying to solve someone else's problem or fear. Now you should be able to speak clearly about what is yours and what is someone else's part of the problem and solution.

3. Check to see whether someone else is controlling you by being upset or threatening to become upset. If you are being controlled, return to step 2 until you can speak calmly and clearly about your responsibilities and boundaries.

4. Check and see whether you are attempting to control others through your threats or upset. If so return to step 2 until you can speak calmly and clearly about your responsibilities and boundaries.

If you still fear and cannot imagine or manage to speak clearly to others about your responsibilities and limits, then we must go deeper and correct problems and develop skills needed for the infant level. With fear-bonds that began as an infant, I can't figure things out on my own, and even if I do, the fear is strong enough that I can't talk freely and openly.

5. Find out what I am really afraid of with help from experienced minds. Often what I am afraid of is not a current-day-reality or what it seems to me. I may think I am afraid I am not doing my job, but I am really afraid someone will be angry or ridicule me. I am afraid I will not survive being ridiculed because of my early life experiences.

6. I must discover who I want with me when I am afraid, and what I want that person to do with or for me. I need someone who can handle the fear without being overwhelmed and help me focus on myself instead of the threat I perceive.

7. I must discover what I really want and what really matters most to me in the current situation so that I can express my goals and values.

8. I must learn to speak about what matters to me, even while I feel afraid, by having someone patiently help me find words I can mean and practice speaking in a low-threat situation, until I am ready to speak of my values, goals and preferences to others who are afraid or of whom I am afraid. This process of defining and expressing our identities gets much easier as our identities mature and become solid. The farther we have grown, the easier it is to change fear-bonds to love-bonds.

Maturity, Recovery and Belonging Work Together

In order for healing and growth to be long lasting, belonging and recovery cannot be separated from maturity. Here is a person's story that illustrates how the three work together.

Jerry entered therapy absolutely hopeless, teetering on the brink of self-destruction, without any support from family. Jerry was middle aged, very wounded and full of fear and anger. In his childhood he had been the victim of physical and emotional abuse by a violent alcoholic father, repeated sexual abuse by neighborhood bullies, and had suffered extreme loss and neglect. He left home at 17 to escape the abuse, moved across the nation, and, having missed his childhood opportunities to develop personal skills, he became engaged in a series of unethical jobs to support himself. By the age of 30 he had developed AIDS, battled continual suicidal urges, and frequently consumed large amounts of hard drugs to numb his pain. He was alone in the world with a new faith in Christ, but was still overwhelmed with a lot of old pain.

During the first months of therapy, although only small pieces of information were safe enough to be shared, a vital process was underway. The joy that the therapist authentically felt in the client's presence and the way she naturally and quite involuntarily communicated, "I'm glad to be with you!" began to fortify the client's joy center, allowing him enough strength to take on some very painful unhealed memories. As the memories surfaced, it became apparent that the client was divided into two battling parts – a vibrant man of God, full of hope and in love with Jesus, and another part, quite sure that the only solution to his miserable existence was death. As Jerry's joy center grew, a previously undiscovered child part also emerged. He was happy and playful, wore bright clothes and smiled with joy. As Jerry allowed God's healing to touch each of these parts, it became obvious that Jerry would not recover alone.

Without a sense of belonging, it became clear that loneliness would dominate his life, leaving him without the strength to grow. A family would be needed.

Prayer was offered that God would provide a spiritual family, and by God's most amazing grace, in only four weeks God orchestrated a miraculous connection. Unaware of Jerry's existence or of his previous history, a woman and her friend sat by Jerry's side at a church they were all visiting. By the end of the service, the women felt compassionately drawn to Jerry, asked if he needed a ride home, and three hours later his new family began emerging! As the women and their husbands enfolded Jerry into their families, Jerry's joy grew, but so did his pain. You see, when a person has received mostly "bad things" in life, and starts getting "good things," it brings up a lot of horrible pain. That is the way A traumas work – good things a person *receives* become reminders of the necessary good things that were *absent* during growing up years, and the pain starts to flood. That was the beginning of what Jerry called his "trauma trip," as he journeyed through the wonderful, yet frightening experience of receiving family love. This part of his recovery was riddled with fear, self-doubt, unbearable pain and more suicidal urges. The journey continued to be arduous but well worth it, and one year after Jerry began counseling, he accurately reported that when he had entered therapy his emotional maturity was about age four. A year later he had progressed well into adolescence. How marvelous, to make up for nine years in 365 days!

As Jerry stepped into adolescence he experienced many of the emotional trademarks of that stage. It must be emphasized here that Jerry was going through *exactly* what teenagers go through, although it was happening years later. Just in case you have forgotten, adolescent feelings are strong, and it was not easy for him to continue his maturity process. It was essential for the therapist to point out how normal these feelings are for teenagers, so that Jerry could appropriately continue his growth without abandoning his faith in God. Having a therapist who understood the process of maturity was critical here.

One year later, Jerry was heading steadily into adulthood. He had received eight promotions at his *ethical* job of two years, could handle emotional pain without using hard drugs, was developing his strengths and talents, and was learning day by day how to receive and give life in authentic relationships, including his relationship with Jesus. His journey had been painfully full of doubts and setbacks, yet the Lord had guided a very delicate weaving of trauma recovery, spiritual adoption and maturity in a way that brought life-giving restoration and healing.

Jerry would not have progressed in therapy if his maturity had stalled at age four, or if he had not received a loving family. There would have been no recovery at all – nothing other than unending pain. As we look next at the process of recovery, let us keep in mind that maturity, spiritual adoption, and trauma recovery all boost each other along as they work together.

Getting Unstuck in Your Maturity Process

1. Intentionally pursue relationships characterized by love bonds that will help you to be all you are created to be (see pages 59-60).
2. Identify a few tasks of maturity that are difficult for you, and prayerfully strive to develop maturity in those areas.
3. Identify past wounds that have stalled your maturity. Seek help from a trusted friend or from a therapist to get you started in the healing and recovery process.

Love Bonds Versus Fear Bonds
In Relationships

LOVE BONDS	FEAR BONDS
1. **Based on love** and characterized by truth, closeness, intimacy, joy, peace, perseverance and authentic giving.	1. **Based on fear** and characterized by pain, humiliation, desperation, shame, guilt, and/or fear of rejection, abandonment, or detrimental consequences.
2. Bond is **desire driven**. (I bond because I want to be with you.)	2. Bond is **avoidance driven**. (I bond because I want to avoid negative feelings or pain.)
3. Love Bonds **grow stronger both when we move closer and when we move farther away.** (When we move closer, I get to know you better. When we move farther away, I am still blessed by the memory of you.)	3. Fear Bonds **only grow stronger by moving closer or by moving farther away.** (The closer we get, the scarier it gets, so I have to avoid the closeness, or the farther away we get, the scarier it gets, so I have to manipulate closeness.)
4. We **can** share **both** positive and negative feelings. The bond is strengthened by this truthful sharing.	4. We **cannot** share **both** positive and negative feelings. The bond is strengthened by 1) avoiding negative or positive feelings, **or** 2) by seeking only negative feelings or seeking only positive feelings.
5. Participants on both ends of the bond benefit; the bond **encourages** all to act like themselves.	5. Participants on only one end of the bond gain advantage; the bond actually **inhibits** people from acting like themselves.
6. **Truth** pervades the relationship.	6. **Deceit** and **pretending** are required.
7. Love Bonds continually **grow and mature** people, equipping them to find their hearts.	7. Fear Bonds increasingly **restrict and stunt** growth, keeping people from finding their hearts.
8. Love Bonds operate from the front of the brain (the joy center), and govern **"How do I act like myself?"**	8. Fear Bonds operate from the back of the brain, and govern **"How do I get what I want?"**

LESSON

5

MATURITY
Part 3

1. Review the "Love Bonds versus Fear Bonds in Relationships" chart. What about this chart impacted you the most, and why? Pg 69
2. Describe in your own words the difference between a fear bond and a love bond. If possible, give an example of each from a relationship you have witnessed. Pg 59-60
3. Describe the differences in how we will motivate ourselves, depending on whether we experience fear bonds or love bonds during our formative years. Pg 59-60
4. Describe the characteristics of fear-bonded individuals. Pg 61
5. Review how an individual with a healthy identity would deal with fear at each of the five levels of maturity. These skills are cumulative, meaning we continue to use them as we add the next levels to our skill set. Indicate which of these you have mastered. What holes do you see? Pg 62-63
6. What about Jerry's story stood out for you, and why? What is your reaction to the fact that in the healing process both joy and pain can increase? Pg 66-68
7. What characteristics would you look for in a person you would trust to develop love bonds with you? What would be your part in finding them? (vs. God's part) Pg 68-69

CHAPTER

3

RECOVERY

As mentioned in the first chapter, we are all broken to some extent, and we all face the challenges of being wounded, divided, isolated and oppressed. We are all in recovery.

Recovery is about exceeding one's current potential, and reaching one's God-intended destiny. The apostle Paul put it this way: "God has made each of us to live a lifestyle that is characterized by doing the good works God has prepared in advance for us to do" (paraphrase of Ephesians 2:10.) Paul is clearly saying that our destiny has been prepared for us by God. Recovery is supposed to help us get past the obstacles created by traumas, so that they will no longer block us from reaching our destiny of doing the important works that God has in mind for us.

Within each person is the natural desire to pursue maturity – to reach the upper limits of one's potential. But life is more than simply reaching one's potential. If that were all, we would be no different than robots, carrying out life as a though it were a series of empty exercises. As spiritual beings, there is a deep longing within each of us to exceed what we could do on our own, to be everything that God intends. That is our destiny and we get there by passing through traumas, gaining as much as we can from each of them. Traumas that do not receive healing will steadily distract our focus and drain our energy away from reaching our destiny.

*Recovery is facing and embracing all the pain in our lives, so that we will gain maximum growth: learning lessons, gaining power, and looking for ways to help others do the same. Those are the goals of recovery, a destiny that is beyond what any person could achieve alone. It takes other people's loving involvement in order to develop our maturity, and it takes God's redemption to bring something good out of our pain. He is working in **everything** for our good – so that we have something extraordinary to give to others.*

Unresolved traumas are serious threats to reaching that destiny, but with God in the middle of recovery, His redemption uses those traumas to achieve the "good works" that God had in mind. God can bring good out of everything, and only He can do that. He knows our identity and works in us to surmount our traumas, so that we can give life to others.

Examples abound. People who conquer a problem often end up getting others unstuck from the same problem. Many helping professionals are people who have been through traumas themselves and are helping others with theirs. An alcoholic founded "Alcoholics Anonymous." God transformed a Christian-killing religious scholar named Saul into the most influential Christian leader of his time. Therapists are often sensitive, caring people, who suffered as children and are now devoted to child protection and adult restoration. Sinners have become evangelists. Parents whose children have died from AIDS are devoting their lives to working with AIDS-affected families. Good comes out of bad. Recovery can lead to redemption.

When the time comes to devote our lives to reaching our destiny, we must be properly prepared. Unless those who surround us provide an environment that encourages trauma recovery, our God-intended destiny will probably not be reached. Recovery must come before the destiny can be reached. This chapter provides a framework to understand woundedness, so that wounded people and those who love them can work together more effectively in recovery.

How Brains Help Us With Traumas

When brains work the way God designed them, joy is in charge. Brains have trauma-solving mechanisms that allow people to move away from the overwhelming effects of traumas and get back to joy, so the traumas can be attended to at a later date. It happens automatically, without thinking.

Here is an illustration. When a veteran, wounded by gunfire during battle, hears a car's muffler crack loudly, the former soldier may find himself flat on the ground, groping for his missing rifle, seeking cover. Without thinking, the protective mechanism has kicked in – the one which meant survival – and his traumatized past becomes his present for a few minutes. He is, right then, living in his pain. We all have moments when we automatically live in our pain, without thinking about it. We need protective mechanisms – sometimes called ego defenses – to promote daily living, and we particularly need them during

..aumas. This veteran used the defense called "dissociation" that helped him forget the terror of the battlefield so that it would not dominate his entire life. In this way, dissociation helped him find his way back to joy.

God, in His wisdom, designed brains to develop enough strength to rebound from traumas. When caretakers provide good early bonding and a safe living environment, a young person's brain can develop so that the correct brain structures become activated and properly aligned. If there is enough strengthening during early years so that brains can work up to potential, people automatically become regulated by joy.

Constructing the Joy Foundation

Being human and wanting joy are inseparable. We are creatures of joy. At its essence, joy is relational. Joy means someone is delighted to be with me and I like it! *Our creator made us with brains that want to operate with joy in charge, and we want our lives to be filled with relationships that lead us to joy.*

The joyful identity region of our brain is also the bonding region. The strength these bonds develop is based on the amount and timing of joy an infant receives. These loving joy bonds also determine the amount of brain growth and strength in the joyful identity region of the brain's right prefrontal cortex. A baby experiences joy through her senses. Taste, smell and temperature determine joy bonds for the first six weeks after birth, while touch brings more joy for the second six weeks. When the visual areas of the brain mature and myelinate at three months, the eyes bring in most joy until hearing voice tones develops at 12 months of age. Each new sense brings a new source of joy for stronger bonds and greater brain development.

The first 12 months are used to build joy-strength brain tissue because this strength is needed to learn how to return to joy from the unhappy emotions of fear, anger, shame, disgust, sadness, and hopeless despair. It is important to learn how to return to joy as soon as the baby has enough strength because of two brain "deadlines" in this next year. At 15 months the limbic system will myelinate and turn on the power for fear and anger. The baby who has not learned to return to joy before the power goes on will have real trouble regulating this intense terror and rage.

The second deadline arrives at 18 months. Until this time the baby's brain has acted like each emotion was in a different brain. But at 18 months, the joyful identity center attempts to grow a ring around all these emotional centers and make one person out of them. The brain will unify control over emotions that are connected with a path back to joy – the other brain centers get left out. This means they are left out of the person's main identity and out of control. For instance, if anger is left out others will notice as she ages that she "acts like a different person" when she gets angry. The goal of maturity, however, is to act like oneself in all emotions and circumstances.

Somewhere between 24 and 36 months, the brain will learn to keep track of our circumstances and surroundings according to time, place, and how we reacted to our surroundings. This is what we normally call conscious memory. With this ability, we can now be ourselves under many different circumstances. We remember so that we can continue being the same person day after day. Around the time the child turns three, the two halves of the brain are joined so that what we feel (the right side) and what we think (the left side) about ourselves and the world will match and be connected.

The normal development and strength of the joyful identity center of the brain is greatly impaired by both "A" and "B" traumas that are experienced during the first three years. During the first year our joy strength is crippled. During the second year the return to joy structures that allow us to function as one person no matter how we feel are broken apart. Traumas in the third year break apart our capacity to stay ourselves in different circumstances over time and what we think about ourselves will not match what we feel or do.

Getting each feeling connected to joy, and setting up joy as the normal state of life is no small task. The parent and the child take about three years spending *lots* of quality time together in order to set up this very important structure.

Here is how that comes about: Joy is intended to be gradually built up to high levels, over time, so that it can become powerful enough to sustain high levels of negative feelings. It is essential for joy to be strong enough to withstand the intensity of trauma-related feelings. Strong feelings, including trauma-related feelings, need to be worked through to a resting point. If strength does not develop, the negatively-powered feelings will not get to a resting point, and there will not be resolution. Until joy is strong enough, and connected to the other feelings, the trauma-related feelings will dominate, and fear will prevail. If there is resolution, the brain goes back to joy. Without resolution, a person ends up getting stuck in fear. The goal of recovery is to build joy that is powerful enough so the other feelings can connect to it and come to a resting place. In this way the brain can work with joy in charge, according to God's design. The emotional pathways can be laid down for effective coping patterns that will last a lifetime.

Jim Wilder has come up with an interesting "Joy Camp" analogy that illustrates the extensive brain development research carried out at leading academic institutions. Dr. Bessel van der Kolk from Harvard, Dr. Allan Schore from UCLA, and Dr. Daniel Siegel from

UCLA have synthesized current developmental research, on which this analogy is based. Anything in the analogy that does not fit with their findings results from our misunderstanding their material.

Joy Camp. The first three months of life are devoted to establishing "Joy Camp" as the base of operations. During those twelve weeks a baby feels joy from being close to the mother. Activities like nursing, rocking, sleeping near the baby or carrying it near her body are very beneficial. This joyful state is the root of all human development. Living in "Joy Camp" is the basis for understanding mother-love, peace, safety and all our treasured experiences. No matter how far we may roam in our lifetime, Joy Camp is where we wish we were each night as we fall asleep. By three months of age the baby has developed enough to picture, in his mind, what the mother feels about the infant. From now on joy becomes very interactive. Until this time, the baby's capacity to feel joy has been very small and easily filled. After three months, however, the main joy structures in the brain begin their serious growth spurt.

Climbing Joy Mountain. At three months of age, babies already have an image of how their mothers see them. Not surprisingly it is stored, without words, as an image of her face. It is also no surprise that climbing Joy Mountain has to wait until the visual areas of the brain develop at three months. By then the visual center has been "hardwired" into place, making vision the dominant sense. What babies begin to look for are eyes that are looking at them with joy. Joy means, "Someone is thrilled to see me."

Joy is the emotion that babies will willingly seek on their own. Because they are motivated to have increasingly higher levels of joy, they will keep working toward joy even when things go wrong. As they climb to higher and higher levels of joy, babies literally build brain capacity. If the infant has the parents' help, the capacity to experience strong joy develops between three and twelve months of age as an infant attempts, repeatedly, to reach higher and higher levels of joy. Each time the baby sees joyful eyes, a face that lights up to see the infant, it makes another attempt to climb Joy Mountain until, by the first birthday, the youngster can regularly reach the top and feel joy as powerfully as a human can feel anything! Hours of this type of practice cause the child to grow a strong and joyful self.

We are creatures of joy, so babies who do not see joy on their mothers' faces, become full of fear. If they attach to a parent who is afraid or angry they learn to watch for threats. If they do not find eyes that are watching them with joy, they will not attach securely, or if there is no one there at all, they monitor the world for anything that could make them feel bad. They develop fear bonds and fear-based identities. They live by avoidance because they have no hope of getting to joy from the fear in which they are stuck. Infants need someone who is paying attention to them and will help them feel joy, or they will fail to thrive. In fact, these babies will not even explore or seek trails that lead back to joy. As they grow older, people who never received love bonds are always searching for someone or something to make them feel better – often drugs, sex, power, abusive relationships or money.

Those with little joy are often overwhelmed, and unable to recover from upset feelings in a timely way. Although it may not be apparent when they are children, as they develop into adults it becomes apparent that their personalities are weaker, and without vigorous workouts on Joy Mountain, their brains are underdeveloped. Weakness in the joyful identity area of the brain has been found in conditions like anxiety, depression, attention deficit disorder, eating disorders, and may also lead to narcissistic, histrionic, obsessive-compulsive, or borderline personality disorders. People with these conditions suffer from an *inability to maintain joy*.

Until the infant has developed a strong self, he may also be *overwhelmed by "too much" joy* every time he gets too high on the mountain. This feels like when we get tickled too much to stand it! Joy turns to pain as a baby reaches "overwhelmed." If a mother is using her baby to make herself happy, she will keep trying to get the baby to smile after the baby has turned away, and this will overwhelm the baby instead of helping him. A good parent will notice that the baby has had too much joy and will look away for a moment to let him rest. When the baby looks back, the parent knows it is time to start climbing again. This process is repeated thousands of times until the baby can reach the top of Joy Mountain. But all these starts and stops on the way up bring hidden bonuses. The baby learns that it can survive being overwhelmed, that it can recover by resting, and that it can eventually return to joy. These steps, repeated many times, teach the child how to avoid pushing others too hard, to be respectful, and to not overwhelm others!

All of us know people who do not know when to stop. These people have great trouble regulating their own feelings, and certainly do not get back to joy very easily. They never learned how to deal with overwhelmed feelings. Their parents did not back off when they reached "overwhelmed." They did not learn to rest and return to joy. This probably happened because the parents needed the child to be happy for them – to make them feel good.

Getting Back to Joy Camp. About the time of the first birthday our hardy little hiker can reliably reach the top of the mountain. This strength will be put to use during the second year of life. During this year, the mother will teach the child how to return to joy from all the unpleasant feelings in life. When a baby has a secure bond with someone who will help it feel better after a painful emotion, it will grow strong and face hardship with hope.

Anyone who has taken young children camping knows how carefully they must be watched to be sure they do not wander off and get lost. When children learn how to get down off the rocks safely, find their way back from the hill on their own, and get back out of the woods without getting lost, parents heave a huge sigh of relief. Their child can now find Joy Camp from anywhere around. Camping becomes safer and far more fun.

In the same way, infants must learn the path back to Joy Camp from all their other feelings. They must be guided from shame back to joy, as well as from disgust, fear, sadness, humiliation and hopeless despair. Once the infant knows the path back, he will not be intimidated by feelings and will not remain stuck. However, the child will only have as much strength to climb back to joy as he developed by climbing Joy Mountain. If the sad feeling, for instance, is higher than the child learned to climb on Joy Mountain, he will run out of strength before he gets back to Joy Camp. From then on he will avoid that feeling instead of resolving it, unless someone teaches him how to return to joy. That is why infants must be guided into these demanding feelings, and back safely, by their parents.

Regulating emotions means being able to feel a negative emotion, even to be overwhelmed by it, and still be able to return to joy. Infants learn this process by imitating others. For example, an eager 15-month-old toddles up to his mommy proudly displaying his dirty hand, which he just successfully stuck into his diaper. Mommy's immediate response is not joy but disgust. The baby senses his mommy's disgust and his immediate response is shame as he runs to hide. His mommy who is mature and sensitive to her baby's needs, recognizes his distress and goes to comfort him. In a matter of moments the mother's face moves from disgust, meets the baby's distress, and then together mommy and baby return to joy.

Mommy's older brain has just taught the infant's younger brain that even when you journey away, there is always a path back to joy. Through this daily repeated process, mommy meets her baby in his negative emotions, comforts him and guides him back to joy. She is not rescuing but simply communicating that she may not like the negative circumstances, but she likes the baby and is still "glad to be with him" as they journey back to joy.

With practice the baby will find paths back to Joy Camp from everywhere – from every difficult and draining feeling and from every bad thing that happens. The strength to feel feelings while knowing the path back to joy builds hope, resilience and confidence. Always returning to joy after a hard feeling teaches satisfaction. When everyone is back in Joy Camp, satisfaction comes from shared joy. This is about returning automatically – not just avoiding a stuck or unpleasant feeling. When people are in Joy Camp together, maturity develops and joy abounds.

According to the developmentally set brain structures, the post-three years are characterized by learning to self-regulate feelings. Traumas cause fractures that become significant blockages to self-regulation. People need loving assistance from others to recover from traumas, and return to self-regulation.

LESSON

6

RECOVERY
Part 1

1. How would you define recovery? List the key characteristics or components of recovery mentioned in pages 71 and 72.
2. Do you believe embracing the pain from past trauma is needed for healing? Why or why not? Pg 72
3. Which of the examples of people who have healed and re-covered from their trauma, and then used the redemption of those experiences to benefit others, are meaningful to you? Describe one example of this from your own life. Pg 72-73
4. Describe what capacity an infant develops at each of the three milestones of the first three years of life, if they receive the joy training they should from their caregivers. Pg 74-75
5. Describe what function is impaired at each year of the child's first three years if they experience trauma. Pg 75-76
6. The book gives a succinct description why we need a strong joy foundation. What about this make sense to you, and what does not? Pg 76-77
7. What effect does it have on infants when their caregiver is focused on his or her own needs, does not know when to stop and consistently overwhelms the infant? Pg 78-79
8. What does "regulating an emotion" mean? Give an example of how a caregiver can assist a young child to return to joy from one of the 6 negative emotions. Pg 80-81

Types of Traumas

People seem to understand that when it comes to medical problems, the correct diagnosis is a must. It is no different when it comes to trauma recovery. In order for us to be successful at recovery, we must first be successful at properly and thoroughly identifying the wounds.

Thirty years of experience in dealing with trauma recovery, has led us at Shepherd's House to see that traumas can be divided into two categories: "Type A" and "Type B" traumas. Identifying these traumas helps us discover the entry point for recovery, and find what it will take to promote healing.

The Absence of Necessary Good Things –
Type A Traumas

Type A traumas come from the absence of good things we should all receive, things that give us emotional stability. These absences create difficulties in relationships. Perhaps an example would help. Years ago, a client of Jim Friesen's was worshipping in his church, and sat a few rows behind him one Sunday morning. Jim's son was about age four at that time, and Jim let the boy stand on a chair while they were singing. He put his arm around his son in a very casual, but warm manner. The client reported later that when she saw the warmth being expressed, a nagging aloneness began to grow inside her, to the point where she had to leave the worship service. The *absence* of love from her father had been painfully with her for years, and the aloneness was re-accessed when she saw the warmth that had not been given to her. That is the way Type A traumas act – the painful feelings begin to emerge when the person sees the good thing that has been absent.

Subsequent relationships are always affected by the *absence* of fulfilling these vital needs. For the person mentioned above, the lack of a warm father led her to distrust men. Thank God, she married an incredibly warm, trustworthy man, and that certainly helped with the Type A wound. But even that warm marital relationship did not heal her wound entirely. Whenever men would show her any warmth, the wound would re-emerge, which would become a sizable hurdle in developing a solid relationship.

The brain structures most seriously affected by Type A traumas are the places where strong emotions are handled. Since the *soul* is primarily devoted to emotions, we can call Type A traumas, *fractures of the soul*. Type A trauma recovery requires enduring love relationships, available to overcome the negative feelings. Then the traumatized person has a chance to express joy and get further along in the maturity process. Developing trust and letting deep feelings emerge are needed to develop enough strength to face the negative feelings. That takes time and it takes the presence of real loving relationships.

Most people find it hard to see that Type A traumas are the cause of their pain, depression, or isolation. These traumas are usually easier to remember than Type B traumas, but are less likely to be given significance. Their importance is denied, leaving persons puzzled about why they feel so awful about themselves, why they are so afraid to trust, or why they feel the continual need to prove their worth. With the significance of the traumas denied, people are at a loss to understand where the disturbing feelings come from. They often can make no sense out of the feelings, and simply place the blame on themselves ("I am defective") or on their Creator ("God made me defective").

Here is an example of a person whose life had been crippled by a Type A trauma. Sue became painfully aware of her own Type A

Type A Trauma

A Type A trauma is harmful by its absence, which causes damage to our emotions. To some degree, one or more of them will typically be found in each stage of our lives, and we all can find at least one Type A trauma wound that needs attention. Looking at the *Maturity Indicators* chart, you will see that a failure by the Family and Community – the middle column – produces a Type A trauma. In fact, *absences* in those areas define what Type A traumas are. Here are a few examples of Type A traumas:

1. Not being cherished and celebrated by one's parents simply by virtue of one's existence.

2. Not having the experience of being a delight.

3. Not having a parent take the time to understand who you are – encouraging you to share who you are, what you think and what you feel.

4. Not receiving large amounts of non-sexual physical nurturing – laps to sit on, arms to hold you, and a willingness to let you go when you have had enough.

5. Not receiving age-appropriate limits and having those limits enforced in ways that do not call your value into question.

6. Not being given adequate food, clothing, shelter, medical and dental care.

7. Not being taught how to do hard things – to problem solve, and to develop persistence.

8. Not given opportunities to develop personal resources and talents.

wound as she was reading about loving parents who showered their children with good things.

Every word brings tears to my eyes. Not tears of joy for those who have made that vital connection with their children and with the Lord, but for myself. Tears that no one cared enough to pray for me, to find out what was going on in my life and in my head, to make the simple sacrifice of time to spend with just me, just because. So alone, so afraid, so swallowed up with the problems of adolescence. Drowning, with no one to notice or care. NO ONE.

Now the pain, apprehension and fear are too much to manage. They are replaced with . . . nothingness – the inability to experience any emotions. You can't just shut one out; if one goes they're all gone. Back to the recesses of your mind, where they wait to be allowed out once again. The few times this is attempted, the wounds too raw, the emotions too brutal, you once again push them into that room. With finality, you lock the door. It's easier, you say, to live without them.

Type A traumas often result in crippling after-effects that are as serious as Sue's. But even the worst wounds can receive healing. It takes *recognizing* the extent of the wound, *facing* the pain, and *welcoming* new life-giving relationships that satisfy the long neglected *absences*.

Therapy can help identify Type A traumas, but it takes loving relationships for recovery. Therapy helps with the traumatizing effects of the *absence* of things that were needed, and loving relationships provide the *presence* of those things so that healing can take place.

The Life Model is not about blaming, but about healing. The purpose of identifying Type A traumas is so they can be healed and our lives can be restored. Have the courage to be honest, so the truth can set you free. God does provide for our needs and He will orchestrate the development of new relationships so that your traumas can be healed. At Shepherd's House we routinely ask people to pray that God will help them identify the people He is bringing into their lives as members of their spiritual family. This is crucial in overcoming the effects of Type A traumas.

Bad Things that Happen – Type B Traumas

Type B traumas come from *bad* things. The brain is seriously effected by "B" traumas in the memory area, so it seems right to call Type B traumas *fractures of the mind*. If the bad events have left unresolved feelings or thoughts, the person cannot get back to Joy Camp. That creates a fracture – a separation. Particular bad events are mercifully forgotten, and amnesia protects the person from re-membering them. Amnesia is an automatic brain function – in-stant forgetting – that can be used protectively after age 3. Before that, the brain cannot establish a time or story line, so memories take a different form.

In order to be clear, here is what is meant when we say that amnesia is "automatic." When a trauma reaches a high enough in-tensity level, it becomes overwhelming. *Before the person is even conscious about what is happening*, the trauma is automatically *for-gotten*, a blank spot in memory appears, and the person has no idea that the traumatic experience ever happened. The person does not choose to forget the overwhelming episode, it is automatically lost to memory before the person can choose to be aware of what was happening. Although amnesia temporarily wipes the memory away, it can be remembered at a later time. If wholeness is to be reached, the bad events need to be recovered and healed, so that the blank spots can be filled in. As is the case for Type A traumas, recovery from Type B traumas can take a long time, although good therapy sessions can speed up "bad event" healing.

Type B Traumas

A Type B trauma is harmful by its *presence*. Having been on the receiving end of the following experiences can create a Type B trauma. There is a range of severity in Type B traumas. It is important to remember that to discount "lesser" traumas is to avoid the truth about how much they hurt, and thereby miss the chance for healing. Avoiding or ignoring wounds do not make them go away. Here are some examples of Type B traumas:

1. Physical abuse, including face slapping, hair pulling, shaking, punching, and tickling a child into hysteria.
2. Any spanking that becomes violent, leaving marks or bruises or emotional scars.
3. Sexual abuse, including inappropriate touching, sexual kissing or hugging, intercourse, oral or anal sex, voyeurism, exhibitionism, or the sharing of the parent's sexual experiences with a child.
4. Verbal abuse or name-calling.
5. Abandonment by a parent.
6. Torture or satanic ritual abuse.
7. Witnessing someone else being abused.

Here is an example of how an unhealed Type B trauma can interrupt a person's life. Lisa was a woman with two young children who kicked her husband out of the house when he made a mistake. It was a serious mistake, to be sure, but it was not the kind of thing that typically ends relationships in a minute's time. In looking at what made her reaction so strong, she became aware that the same strong feeling had been there when she was young. With some focused attention on where that feeling was coming from, the memory of a Type B trauma came up, quite forcefully, in her mind. There was a time when she had complete trust in her stepfather, until one night he came into her room and molested her. Lisa continued to let the memory come up, and she remembered that her reaction to him had been rage – she was furious, and told her mother what had happened. The stepfather was then sent out of the home immediately, and the relationship ended right there.

After recognizing that the husband's mistake had touched off powerful feelings that were attached to the stepfather's behavior, Lisa's surprisingly strong reaction made more sense. The unhealed wound, which had remained forgotten until this time, generated intense feelings as soon as it was touched off. The feelings initially spilled over onto the husband, but with proper attention, the wound was healed. That particular strong reaction no longer interrupted her relationship with her husband after the healing took place.

Therapy can assist in uncovering Type B traumas, many of which remain lost to the person's conscious memory well into adulthood. We have found that remembering and healing the trauma is necessary, or the wound will continue to fester. It usually takes more than making a general prayer that the Lord will cover everything painful in a person's past. It takes finding the wound, opening the hurt feeling enough to understand the effect of the trauma, and praying that the Lord will bring full healing to the recovered memory.

Healing for Woundedness

God is so good, and at Shepherd's House we share people's joy of witnessing restoration as God directs and provides healing for both A and B traumas. Following is an account of a particular session that portrays how healing for both kinds of traumas can be approached.

Karl had been led by a friend to seek help at Shepherd's House. That is community in action. Karl's friend was involved in getting him help, and it was essential to have his wife there during this session as his therapy partner. She was the only one who could give him what his heart needed right then.

A feeling had been lurking near the surface since Karl's previous session, a feeling that suggested he was not worth enough to enjoy a nice meal at a restaurant. He sensed he was a younger person while the feeling began to surface during this session, and Karl was asked if he could let the young part of him open up and tell us what was going wrong.

In a young voice, Karl said he was afraid of the dark, afraid of spiders, afraid of being locked in a closet, and afraid of his mother's boyfriend. "Anything else?" He was also afraid of his mother. For about five minutes Karl continued in a young voice and recounted a few episodes that took place when he was about age four. Those were B traumas – bad things, things which we would call child abuse. Karl was consciously remembering these very upsetting events for the first time since they had happened. It was a relief for the young part of Karl to express in words the awful events that had been quietly painful for years. The feelings from those events had recently been crowding into his life – they were the fears he struggled with about not deserving to go out to eat. One of the events he remembered was precisely that. He had been locked in a closet while his mother and her boyfriend went out for dinner! The mother even said something about Karl not being worth anything, otherwise they would have taken him along! Prayer for healing those memories had a calming effect, and the lie was broken that Karl was not important.

But joy had not yet been reached. He was afraid his mother would never come back. Evidently, a Type A trauma was part of the picture – his mother did not convey to the young Karl that he could rely on her. He did not sense he *belonged* to her. A prayer for healing of memories would not be enough to fill the void that was created by the absence of love by the mother. It would take real people, and the right real person was sitting next to Karl. His wife put her arms around him and told him very compassionately that they belonged together – the Lord put them together, and he could rely on her. After prayer for the "belongingness wound," and a prayer to bless their relationship, joy was reached. His wife was delighted to be with him, and that brought the *presence* of joy into the *absence* of belonging that he had grown up with. Young Karl, for the first time, had found a way back to Joy Camp! Every feeling can be connected to joy, whether it resulted from A or B traumas. God's healing provided the "joy connection" for Karl, and it also required a person whom God had put in his life, to become part of his recovery.

Karl had been to pastoral counselors and Christian therapists, and had been seeking help for about 25 years! Since his mid-teen years he had been fighting feelings that did not resolve. He was able to live, but the struggle had been fierce and life-threatening for years. His marriage and career had suffered. Tragically, Karl is one of countless persons whose quest to resolve painful feelings has failed – until now. *In order to resolve feelings that come from Type B traumas, the memory that contains the feelings must be uncovered. A general prayer for healing everything in the person's past does not typically help. The specific wound needs to be opened up in the presence of caring persons, along with a prayer for healing. Anything else will achieve only temporary relief, because the wound will continue to fester until it is specifically addressed.*

Psychology can teach us how to find these hidden wounds, but it takes more than *discovering* the problem to solve it. God is needed to *heal* the uncovered wounds. Without His touch, the search for help will fail. It is also clear that without loving relationships, there would not be enough human support for recovery. It takes God and it takes His family.

Different Kinds of Fractures

Karl's wounds had produced the kind of fracture that results in amnesia – terrifying, overwhelming feelings. They overwhelmed him while he was locked in the closet, and resulted in dissociation. A simple way to think about dissociation is to think of it as instant forgetting – amnesia, or a *fractured mind*. The brain has a switch that can deal with overwhelming feelings, and record them in a place that does not contact the conscious memory. That is hugely beneficial at the time. The young Karl could head off for school in the morning, not needing to struggle with the memory of being locked in the closet the night before. Nor did he need to fear coming home because he, literally, did not remember the closet trauma while he was on his way home. This was a Type B trauma that resulted in a fracture of Karl's mind. This event had been lost to his conscious memory through dissociation.

That is the way amnesia works – it is a sane way to deal with events that are crazy-making. God created amnesia to protect souls from being overwhelmed, which allows them to continue to live apart from the hurt. Karl's trauma history produced enough fractures to give quite a few "child parts" a place in his life. He was not conscious of these "child parts," but when he could, in later years feel their powerful, negative feelings, Karl's adult life was seriously interrupted. Rotating the wounded child parts into consciousness during therapy gave us a chance to heal their woundedness, and to show these parts how to get to Joy Camp. It is a tremendous relief for people like Karl to have hidden wounds healed. Joy is the automatic result.

This session also reveals how another important protective mechanism works – repression. It is the gradual forgetting of conscious material. There was a whole chapter of Karl's life that was full of upsetting, abandonment-related experiences with his mother, but these were not severe enough to reach his "overwhelming switch" (dissociation). His conscious memory retained all those events, which had "abandonment" written all over them. But, through repression, he lost contact with how painful they really were. Repression helped him convince himself that the feelings were not so bad.

The mind works very hard to shape feelings, to make life a little more livable. Rationalization, sublimation and the rest of the ego defenses we all read about in "Introduction to Psychology" classes serve that purpose. They help us deal with difficult feelings. Repression is a defense that lets us forget, gradually, just how upsetting things were. Karl was protected from the power of a Type A trauma by losing an accurate memory of the abandonment events, and forgetting that he had been abandoned helped him in his struggle with self-worth. He forgot just how painful things were, but he could not avoid the hole in his life, that resulted because of the A trauma – he did not belong. Replacing the "belongingless" chapter in his life with real belongingness, helped Karl with his self-worth. His wife helped him with what he had missed growing up. She helped him overcome the effects of a *fractured soul*.

Many people are crying out to belong. They need a spiritual family, which is explained more fully in Chapter 4. If they get prayer from their Christian friends without belonging, as had been the case for Karl, the B traumas would feel a little better, but resolution would still be absent. No wonder we are commended to *both* pray and love – but not one without the other.

Let us take a look at how healing for different kinds of traumas often misfires in the church setting. People with Type A traumas can have a particularly hard time in church services. Other people get healing for Type B traumas, which can be amazingly quick because B traumas often cover just one event, and one brief span of time. Relief for this kind of healing is encouraging to many, but it is discouraging for the people who have A traumas. They may ask the Lord, "Why me? Other people are getting better and feeling joy, but why not me? Don't you love me, God, or are Your promises only for other people? Is something wrong with me? Am I bad?" Things get worse when fellow church members try to treat them like "Type B trauma people." The result is that the "Type A trauma people" come to believe they do not fit in church with these people because their recovery is not quick, and they get a tragic sense that they do not belong! Isolation and rejection are often at the root of their trauma history already, and with pressure to get quick healing for deep wounds, they fail, and again feel isolation and rejection. This is not the way it should be. Real people are needed to restore the souls of people with Type A traumas, and the restoration will take more than a few minutes.

It is important to include another example. As was the case with Karl, healing the B traumas helped a lot, but Type A healing was also needed in order for this person to be whole. There are people who may go up to the front of the church after worship services for prayer. They get help for Type B wounds, and that brings relief for the B wounds, but later they come in touch with the more deeply painful Type A wounds, which do not feel much better because of prayers alone. They may conclude that they need to go back for prayer repeatedly, because at least that makes them feel better for a while. Such thinking will not bring the desired results. If they continue to live with unhealed Type A wounds, they will not feel much better for very long, until real people begin to love them enough to make up for the good stuff, which was missing in their growing-up years. They will not sense that they belong until they become connected to the people God brings into their lives. As was mentioned in Chapter 1, it is important to know what kind of a wound the person has, or the approach to healing will likely fail.

LESSON

7

RECOVERY
Part 2

1. What did you learn about Type A trauma from the story of the woman who recognized her pain regarding what she did not receive from her father? What about her response made sense to you? Pg 83-84

2. Read the list of examples of Type A traumas. What Type A traumas can you identify in your life? Which of the big six feelings does this bring up for you? Pg 85*

3. What are the three factors involved in recovery from Type A traumas?   P 84-86

4. What did you learn from reading Lisa's story that helped you better understand the amnesia or dissociation that can result from Type B trauma? Pg 88-89

5. Read the list of examples of Type B traumas. What Type B traumas can you identify in your life? Which of the big six feelings does this bring up for you? Pg 88*

6. What factors are needed to heal Type B trauma? Pg 87-92

7. Since the process and duration of healing are different for Type A and Type B traumas, how can these differences negatively impact the Type B trauma survivor in the church community? Pg 94-95

* Remember that group members may choose not to share the answers to any questions they do not feel ready to share. Members should gently share feelings rather than details of Type B traumas.

Assessing Your Dividedness

The kind of fracturing, or dividedness, which we found in Karl is *rotating dividedness*. This has been called "Multiple Personality Disorder" and is now called "Dissociative Identity Disorder" in the scientific community. It results when traumas reach the overwhelming level, dissociation occurs, and the personality is fractured into distinctive parts.[3] There may or may not be amnesia, but there is always separation between the feeling states, or parts, and there are very negative feelings stored in some of the parts. Sadly, not all of the feelings in these parts get connected to Joy Camp, and therefore they remain stuck. When the stuck parts rotate out, the people remain in fear because the path to Joy Camp is not found. *The best therapy gets all parts of the person connected to joy, so that the joy area of the brain can take over again. That is the way self-regulation is established.*

A second kind of dividedness can be referred to as *alternating dividedness*, which is what we see in people with drug and alcohol abuse problems, sexual addictions, and what therapists have called "borderline disorder." This is what happens in *alternating dividedness* – people go back and forth between the part of them that is successful and the part that is wounded. The defeating aspect of *alternating dividedness* is that the successes do not get very far because the wounds keep interfering. Whenever hurt comes up, the learned pattern happens automatically – alcohol abuse, eating disorders, physically abusive behavior, or some other response that has unhealthy side effects. These unhealthy responses to pain were learned during childhood, and the person senses that there is no other way to respond when the unhealthy patterns begin. As is the case for

---

[3] See *Uncovering the Mystery of MPD* and *More than Survivors: Conversations with Multiple Personality Clients*, by Jim Friesen, for more information about dividedness and dissociation.

rotating dividedness, it is an automatic response, in that there is no conscious decision to rotate – it just happens. Tragically, the person starts to believe that there is no way to control the problem, the bad outcomes increase, and the successful outcomes do not.

Here is how the life of a person with *alternating dividedness* typically looks. They have a significant Type A wound in childhood and a few Type B wounds as well, which pose a significant block to maturity. Typically, Type A woundedness does not get addressed in church, in traditional therapy, or in most formal approaches to the problem. The perplexing thing is that these people have a "good side," but the wounded side is thought of as a "bad side." How defeating that is! The talents are undeveloped, and the bad self-image is often deeply entrenched. It is not bad, just wounded. *We should not focus on controlling that part, but on healing it.* It usually does not help people with *alternating dividedness* to go to groups, if they show up with their "good-intentioned" side. They need to show up in their wounded side and get some healing for the woundedness, or no progress can be expected. The same is true for those in therapy. If they come into therapy full of smiles, talking about the troubles they *had last week*, but do not bring along painful feelings, they can expect no progress. Healing for *alternating dividedness* means getting into the woundedness, while in the presence of real people who love them just as they are – people who know that healing for woundedness can take time, and invest the time that is needed.

A third kind of dividedness can be called *reacting dividedness*. These people seem very solid most of the time, but once in a while they just lose control. Even when they return to their solid selves again, they can be dangerous when they react, and their relationships can become unstable. Here is how to understand them. They have some unresolved traumas, both A and B, which are mostly controlled, but when strong feelings surface, they find themselves reacting from the build-up of unresolved feelings that have been stored up inside. Surprised at the intensity of their own reaction, they can lose confidence and start isolating, or get severely depressed and hopeless.

As stated in Chapter 1, we are all divided to some degree, but we do not need to stay stuck. You have one or more of the three kinds of dividedness mentioned, depending on your trauma history. It may help you immensely to identify your kind of dividedness, if you are going to reach your God-given potential. Take time to understand your traumas, and to understand your dividedness. God wants to bring good out of whatever has kept you stuck.

Spiritual Interventions

For many years there have been questions raised about the role of prayer, and other spiritual interventions, in trauma recovery. In addition to the clinical work at Shepherd's House, from which we have learned about spiritual interventions first-hand, Jim Friesen conducted some research that directly addresses these questions. Two studies he carried out seem important to mention at this point, because they show that many Christian therapists use spiritual interventions, and *know* that they are very effective.

Study #1 was a survey conducted with 66 Christian therapists who work with trauma recovery clients, in order to find out which spiritual interventions they used. Over 40 identifiable interventions were found, and 10 of them were found to be used by more than 90% of the respondents, showing very consistent experiences among the therapists:

1. Praying during sessions.
2. Actively seeking to bring dissociated personality parts into a relationship with God.
3. Asking God to guide in uncovering traumatic memories.

4. Binding demons that may interfere during sessions.
5. Praying for healing of traumatic memories after they emerge.
6. Asking for intercessory prayer back-up.
7. Teaching dissociated parts how to use their spiritual power.
8. Inviting therapy partners to attend sessions.
9. Maintaining contact with the client's spiritual family.
10. Casting out demons during sessions.

Study #2 followed up on the first study, and asked which spiritual interventions were found to be effective. Again, Christian therapists who do trauma recovery work were surveyed, and 102 questionnaires were returned. Following are the items that were rated very effective more than half the time, starting with the item that was rated highest:

1. Intercessory prayer back-up for particular sessions.
2. Praying for a client's protection, outside of therapy.
3. Prayer for healing of traumatic memories.
4. Prayer with clients during sessions.
5. Praying for protection of a client, during a session.
6. In agreement with the client, asking God, aloud, for direction when an obstacle is found during a session.
7. Breaking curses or generational ties placed on a client.
8. Asking God to send angels for protection or ministry during sessions.
9. Seeking to bring dissociated personality parts into relationships with God.
10. Asking God, in silent prayer, for direction when an obstacle is found.
11. Using "offense" prayers outside of sessions, to block evil spirits from carrying out assignments, and to block the people who sent them from gaining future access to power from darkness.

12. Quoting scripture to break therapeutic impasses – strongholds.
13. In agreement with the client, asking God to guide in uncovering traumatic memories.
14. Teaching dissociated parts how to use their spiritual power for protection from spiritual harassment, including casting out demons.
15. Using "offense" prayers, during sessions, to block evil spirits from carrying out assignments, and to block the people who sent them from gaining future access to power from darkness.
16. Asking God, aloud, to bind demonic interference during a session.
17. Casting out demons, aloud, during a session.
18. Silently seeking words of knowledge, or an image from God, concerning clients during sessions.
19. Reading scripture, as part of worship and praise during sessions.
20. Teaching dissociated personality parts to pray.
21. Asking the Lord to uncover programming.

These two studies indicate very strongly that *it is routinely a standard of practice for Christian therapists to pray, and to expect that God will be very active in the therapy they carry out.* It is clear that certain interventions may be more appropriate than others. However, the overarching conclusion we must draw from these results is this: *Prayer works and prayer is needed!*

The Life Model agrees with these findings. Developmental psychology has shown us a great deal about helping people to make gains in maturity. Family therapy and community psychology, along with medical research, have also made important contributions to *The Life Model.* As Christians, we believe that God created everything just as it should be, including humans, and we know that psychology is dedicated to finding out as much as possible about humankind. Psychology certainly has made enormous contributions. However, psychology is limited in that it is restricted to human observation, and spirituality is not confined in that way. Here is a simple guideline: *Psychology is a good thing. It helps us know what to pray for.*

The two studies discussed above highlight how to pray more effectively in therapy. In every part of *The Life Model* – in discovering maturity deficits, in resolving traumatic memories, and in finding God's direction for spiritual adoption – we must keep turning to God for guidance and wisdom, as well as for healing and protection.

Breaking the Power of Lies

Dividedness and woundedness keep people stuck when a person lives life on the basis of the lies that result from traumas. Traumatic events often bring a two-fold destructive legacy into a person's life – there is a wound and there is a lie, and people suffer because of both. Both need to be properly taken care of before a person can live from the heart that Jesus gave them. In order for you to live from your heart, you must live in truth, and the lies that are a part of your hurt will need to be broken. When your life is spent living from your hurt, *that means the lies are directing your life.*

Of the lies that endure as after-affects of traumas, a very common serious lie is this: "You will never get better." Other widespread lies are, "God may help others but He will not help you," "You are bad," "You deserve to suffer for the rest of your life," and "You will never be safe." The lies are tailored to each particular person and to each trauma, but they are all lies, and they keep people living from their hurts instead of their hearts.

The "you-will-never-get-better" lie typically becomes attached to traumas that are physically painful for hours and hours, with the trauma happening periodically again. The pain seems virtually unstoppable, and there is nothing the person can do to keep it from happening again. Those become powerful moments in the person's life, when that lie seemed true. The moment was absolutely overwhelming, which added to the lie that *"you will never get better."* Breaking the lie needs to be a part of healing for the wound.

Typically the particular trauma needs to be discovered and receive healing before the lie can be broken. This must happen because if the wound remains unhealed, the lie can reattach itself. If the person has a place inside where the memory of the "never-getting-better" wound is still festering, the lie will not be broken. Until healing, the lie can stay alive – "You will *never* get better." After the traumatic event has been uncovered and healed, the lie will be exposed. Then it needs to be renounced, and replaced with the truth.

As the Bible says, "The weapons we fight with are not the weapons of the world. On the contrary, they have divine power to demolish strongholds [lies]. We demolish arguments and every pretension that sets itself up against the knowledge of God, and we take captive every thought to make it obedient to Christ" (II Corinthians 10:4-5). The presence of Jesus, the guidance of the Holy Spirit or the quoting of relevant scriptures exposes and demolishes the lie.

Scriptures like "I can do everything through [Christ] who gives me strength" (Philippians 4:13); "My God will meet all your needs according to his glorious riches in Christ Jesus" (Philippians 4:19); and "[Jesus said] I have come that [you] may have life, and have it to the full" (John 10:10), are all examples of powerful lie breakers. Jesus exposes and expels the lie. The presence of Jesus in a wound often results in the breaking and removing of the demonic influence attached to that wound, and establishes His truth where the lie once was.

After the lies have been broken the lessons can be learned which will lead you to your destiny, lessons that are based on Scripture. "I am not doomed to suffer for the rest of my life. God will meet my needs. There are things I can do, with Christ in me, to live my life to the full." The lessons lead to more satisfaction than expected, because people underestimate how good it is to live with joy in charge instead of fear. These lessons need to be put into practice by participating in the family of God. We cannot get our needs met any other way – it has to be real life with real people. Therapy alone is not enough. God wants to provide strength and meets our needs through the people He puts in our lives. They become our adopted, spiritual family.

Here is an account of a Shepherd's House client, and her experience with trauma recovery.

A client came in with a fervent love for Jesus, but she also had a nagging desire to kill herself. Although she was a godly woman who had been brought to salvation and sobriety almost 10 years earlier, her unresolved wounds, coupled with the lies that Satan had attached to the wounds, were cutting off much of her joy in the Lord, leaving her very depressed and highly suicidal.

As she met with her therapist week after week, God was faithful in directing them to the wounds that needed healing, and one by one, Satan's lies – the deceitful messages that led her away from the truth about herself and about God – were also exposed. She had been labeled "ugly" as a small child, was convinced that she was "nothing" as a Junior Higher, and got into the "wrong crowd" as a High Schooler, losing one baby to abortion and another to an unofficial adoption. She had battled drug addictions for 20 years, and had been battered by a violent boyfriend. Attached to those wounds were messages like, "You always will be worth nothing;" and "You must die, so commit suicide to make up for the unforgivable sin of abortion."

As each wound was uncovered, she and her counselor prayed that God's power would heal each wound. As each lie was discovered she relied on God's truth and wisdom to break the power of Satan's lies.

As the client honestly revealed herself, she and her counselor also identified her rotating dividedness. She had been fragmented into at least three distinguishable parts – a frightened, sad child; a punishing, suicidal self; and a strong, faithful woman of God. By working to heal and to integrate these parts, the client found new strength and wholeness.

Six months into treatment, an unexpected trauma broadsided her. Amazingly enough, however, since significant wounds had been healed and destructive lies had been broken, the client's suicidal feelings had disappeared entirely, and her wholeness allowed her to battle the new trauma with a strength that she had never experienced before.

As she appropriately mourned and grieved her new loss, she also began living from the heart Jesus gave her, as the woman that God had created her to be. This positioned her to continue working on maturity tasks, like learning to take care of herself. She stepped forward with great courage, excited to learn new things that enabled her to more fully receive and give life as well as more consistently experience God and His joy!

Guidelines for Getting Unstuck in Recovery

1. Identify any Type A and Type B traumas in your life in order to clarify what resources you will need for healing. For example, Type A traumas require caring people to make up for the deficits you suffered as a child. Type B wounds require healing, and both types of traumas leave lies, which need to be exposed, broken and replaced with the truth.

2. Identify specific emotions that you get stuck in, or those that you work extra hard to avoid. Intentionally allow yourself to experience these, and then look for ways to get back to joy, primarily by receiving love and support from those close to you, and by using the lessons that maturity has taught you.

3. Identify the lies that were imbedded with the wounds that may be unhealed in your life. Actively bring God's truth to break the power of the lie. To know the truth allows one to be set free and to live in freedom.

4. Seek to be covered in prayer by others. Pray that God will heal your wounds, break the lies, and replace them with His truth.

LESSON

8

RECOVERY
Part 3

1. What is your response to reading that there is empirical research that concludes that the use of prayer in therapy sessions is not only common, but also effective? Pg 99-101
2. As you read the lists of prayer interventions from the two studies, which of these might be beneficial to incorporate into your own recovery? Pg 99-101
3. As you read the examples of lies, what are some of the lies you have believed as a result of your trauma experience? Pg 102-105
4. Describe how the circumstances and events of a particular trauma result in the content of the lie matching that experience. Pg 102-103
5. What is your understanding of why the specific trauma that formed the lie must be healed before the lie can be permanently broken? Pg 103-105
6. Describe the role and the importance that other people play in the healing process after the lies have been broken. Pg 104
7. What did you learn about the process of healing from reading the story of the Shepherd's House client? Pg 104-105
8. Look at the "Guidelines for Getting Unstuck in Recovery." Where are you in the process of doing each of these healing activities? Pg 106

CHAPTER

4

BELONGING

Life is about receiving and giving – reaching one's destiny, and helping others reach theirs. Living from the heart Jesus gave you requires more than receiving life's essentials from family members only – it also takes a community. It takes belonging to a caring family and to a community of caring men and women who can guide and protect you.

In fact, each girl and boy needs a few caretakers from each gender. We become mature by *receiving* what we need at the right time in our development, primarily from parents and other significant people in our community. These people are to be "mirrors" through which God shows us who we are and what we can become. But every mirror is a little damaged or warped, so everyone needs more than one mirror to get an accurate image. Because even good parents cannot possibly fill in all the gaps and will, no doubt, miss something, we need more than two parents to act as mirrors for us. Without these extra mirrors, we probably will not get to know our true selves. In fact, we will stay stuck at some level of development that is still waiting to grow, be encouraged and be nurtured.

Here is how one community significantly contributed to a young man's life. Early in his elementary school years he was repeatedly humiliated in front of his classmates by the man who was his principal. The joy of being with others at school, or finding protection from authority figures was lost. Being very small and hurt, with no way to protect himself, he began to behave defiantly against the principal, who punished him abusively. For about eight years, that boy remained stuck in his identity as a troublemaker. He grew into the role, and kept acting defiantly against male authority figures. A prominent member of the community had traumatized the boy, and for a few years the boy incorrectly acted out his defiance against other authority figures in the community who received the anger that should have been directed towards the abusive principal.

Things began to turn around early in his teenage years. He gained some relief when he told his parents what had happened with the principal. For the first time, he felt totally accepted, and had a chance to do better. He was starting to rediscover his true self again, a process which had been cut off by the abusive principal. But the improved relationship with his parents was not enough to help him reverse his "troublemaker" identity. During the whole span of his school years, his piano teacher – a woman – steadily helped him develop his talents, and in high school his youth group leader – a man – brought out these talents. All the while, his parents were positively involved, but it became clear that encouraging this dynamic and gifted young man to find his true identity took a community of caring men and women and it also required affirming friends. Caring teachers and sports mentors who saw that this boy had potential that needed to be developed, and affirming friends from both genders were needed to get him unstuck and reconnected to his joy so he could discover the heart that Jesus gave him. Passing on what he learned to other teens was also important. Becoming a leader in his school and in his youth group is how he contributed to his community. The abuse came from within his community, but so did the recovery. That is how it should be.

Particularly during teenage years people need other adults, in addition to their parents, to encourage and develop their identities and their talents. They need older people to learn from, they need friends to encourage them, and they need younger children to teach. Maturing means modeling after those who have matured, and modeling for those who are younger. It takes belonging to a caring family and to a caring community. It takes receiving from them and giving to them. It takes a lifetime, and there can be joy all along the way.

Spiritual Adoption

Joining the family of God always involves brokenness. We come to the place where we face the reality that without God's involvement we have no hope. It is a matter of irrevocable need. With Him there is life. All other roads lead to death.

Spiritual adoption is building bonds in relationships that God ordains.[4] When we turn our lives over to Him, He brings people into our lives to be members of our eternal family. He ordains the adoptive relationships, and it remains for us to grow the relation-

---

[4] See *The Red Dragon Cast Down*, by Jim Wilder, for more information about spiritual adoption.

ships in ways that are pleasing to Him. In fact, His design for adoptive relationships shows up throughout the Bible, in stories and in teachings. Following are three examples that illustrate how adoption is included as a part of His design for living.

1. Jesus promises in Mark 10:29-30 that ". . . no one who has left home or brothers or sisters or mother or father or children or fields for me and the gospel will fail to receive a hundred times as much in this present age (homes, brothers, sisters, mothers, children and fields . . .) and in the age to come, eternal life."
2. King David, in Psalm 68:5-6, extols God, who is "a father to the fatherless, a defender of widows, . . . [and] sets the lonely in families."

The apostle Paul's extensive teaching to the Corinthian believers also describes the adoptive nature of relationships in the family of God. "Even though you have ten thousand guardians in Christ, you do not have many fathers, for in Christ Jesus I became your father through the gospel. Therefore I urge you to imitate me. For this reason I am sending to you Timothy, my son whom I love, who is faithful in the Lord. He will remind you of my way of life in Christ Jesus, which agrees with what I teach everywhere in every church" (I Corinthians 4:15-17). This text suggests that to live as fathers and sons, and brothers and sisters in Christ, was the style of living taught by Paul in the early church, which is not different from what we saw in the texts cited from Jesus and from David.

When we say "Yes" to Jesus, we can expect that He will place us in families. It remains for us to develop bonds of love in these relationships so that we can receive and give the love He has put in our hearts.

When we join His family, we acknowledge that we need His glorious riches to strengthen us in our inner being (see Ephesians 3:16-19), and we need to be vitally connected to the people in His family. The book of Ephesians emphasizes the unity of the family of God, serving each other wholeheartedly, and building each other up according to their needs. We all start out broken, and we all depend on His family to boost the transformation process for each of us, so that we can grow a joyful identity.

In cases where our biological family members are also in our spiritual family, that is a blessing. But even when that is the case, God will choose particular people from His community to assist our growth, and they will also become family members to us. We will be able to look to them for guidance on a regular basis, because of the unity we enjoy, because of our desire to serve each other, and because of the goal to build each other up by meeting needs. Entering God's family involves spiritual adoption. We come into it and we receive. Then we give.

The family of God is made up of the people God brings into your life who give you what your heart needs. To take the step of faith, and say, "Yes, Master, I will follow you," means that God will give you membership in His family. He draws the people close to you who will give you what your heart needs. They are intended to make available to you the fulfillment of your belongingness needs. You will learn to help them satisfy their belongingness needs too, as your maturity grows.

The concept of spiritual adoption is not a case of being related to everyone in your church! Of course, you share a bond in Christ, but that is not the way we think about "the family of God" at Shepherd's House. It would be impossible to be close to that many people. Fellow church-goers are people in your extended spiritual family, but God will probably select a few of them to give you what your heart needs. God often picks out people to be your spiritual family members from those you get to know in small groups, like choirs, Sunday school classes, or Bible studies. They are people you may not think of as "relatives" at first. However, over time, it gradually becomes evident that they have been adopted into your family, even though you were not aware of it as it was beginning to happen. The key experience of adoption is that God's redemption is going on, and you are part of it! You are helping other people to deepen their sense of belonging, and to make gains in maturity, so that they can become everything that God had in mind for them.

Some people have been raised in families that are quite different from what is described in biblical guidelines. These people often move into their adult years alone, low in people skills, lacking maturity, and without the correct family dynamics in place to overcome their deficits. The biological parents may have been severely dysfunctional or absent, and there may have been no community to help them mature in their growing up years. These people have very little chance of accomplishing certain maturity tasks. Spiritual adoption is an opportunity for the family of God to fill a very big void in people's lives, and God will be needed to orchestrate all the details. Here is an example of such an adoption.

We got a note at Shepherd's House, from a woman who asked if we knew a good therapist in her area – a state half way across the country. Even though we did not, we gave her a phone number of an organization with a referral list of therapists all over the country, hoping to help her find a therapist not too far from home. Months later, we received a note of thanks and praise to God who had led her to the therapist she needed, which also turned out to involve spiritual adoption! After finding that two therapists from the referral list did not have room or time for her, she wrote to us that the Lord shut all other doors so that she would, through a series of unlikely events, end up seeing the doctor God had in mind. He had lots of experience in treating her condition – rotating dividedness – and lowered his price so she could afford to see him regularly. Her note included this: "We finally got an ideal dad," and she drew a happy face at the end of that sentence. Even though things were not yet fully worked out, she said she was thankful for the healing she had already received. She continued, "I know the Lord can do anything. If not, he wouldn't have bothered to take me to this doctor." The letter concluded with a request for continued prayer, and this blessing. "May God's loving kindness, and the transforming power of His presence be manifested in your midst!!" We at Shepherd's House are thankful, too, because God used us along her pathway to adoption by a person who could give her what her heart needed.

When the family of God is working correctly, this kind of adoption is not rare. The Bible is clear. "Religion that God our Father accepts as pure and faultless is this: to look after orphans and widows in their distress, and to keep oneself from being polluted by the world" (James 1:27).

Levels of Adoption

Spiritual adoption happens in many ways, and is only evident to those looking for it. It is not "role playing," in order to give the person a taste of what it is like to have a family member. It is real, it is authentic and it is always part of God's redemptive plan. Spiritual adoption is a lasting relationship that is ordained by God, and should not be treated lightly.

Spiritual adoption allows redemption to happen by having other people stand in to fill the gaps left in a person's life by his biological family. With these gaps left open, the person will not sense they belong to a caring family. A person may only need a mother, or a father, or perhaps a sister or brother. Sometimes they may need a set of replacement parents. An adoptive person becomes established at one of three levels – as a *stand-in* family member (for help with a particular occasion or period of time), a *supplemental* family member (for someone who received good things from their parents but was still lacking in some areas), or a *replacement* family member. People at the first two levels are usually adopted as brothers or sis-

The Life Changing Revelation

"Religion that God our Father accepts as pure and faultless is this: to look after orphans and widows in their distress, and to keep oneself from being polluted by the world" (James 1:27).

Let us explain how this Bible verse became life changing to all of us at Shepherd's House. After about twenty years of dealing with wounded hearts, we finally realized that the one thing that severely wounded people had in common was that they have been "cut off" from the support of their biological families by death, dysfunction or distance. It took us years to discover this, but once we did, the truth became glaring. Then the revelation hit! The group we had identified as being especially wounded – those cut off from the support of their biological families – were the very group God was commanding us in the Bible to take very special care of: "widows, orphans and strangers." What do these groups of people have in common? They are not part of a family because they have been cut off by death, dysfunction or distance. It took about 20 years to make a discovery that God had been trying to tell us for thousands of years. Wounded people need real, live, loving families. That is what the family of God is supposed to be. For severely wounded people, spiritual adoption means the difference between life and death, between recovery and destitution. It takes us so long to learn God's lessons, but once we learn, we dare not ignore them.

ters, or aunts or uncles, but at the third level we almost always find that adoptive parent relationships are needed.

There are times when people find themselves grasping to manage their lives, and need assistance in some particular way. Perhaps a divorced person cannot figure out how to develop a budget, fix a clothes dryer or how to negotiate car repairs with a local mechanic. She may need someone to help her get unstuck. Those are examples of spiritual adoption at the *stand-in* level. For people who are broken-hearted, weak or wounded, it often takes quite a few willing spiritual family members to stand in to help them with a host of problems that many of us can solve with very little effort. Particularly at moments like that, it becomes crystal clear that people who have already received, get a ton of enjoyment from giving, and those who receive profit immensely. Receiving and giving come to life at the *stand-in* level of adoption.

Most of us can identify at least one *supplemental* family member whom God has brought into our lives. People often become *supplemental* family members as the result of getting involved in an intimate group like at our work place, a Sunday school class or a Bible study group. Developing friendships with people in this way certainly allows for closeness to grow. Most of us can look back and remember times when people who are now important to us, people we met in these kinds of groups, began to relate in a way that became more and more like family members. This is how God supplies needs, through spiritual adoption at the *supplemental* level. In many cases these are the people we now invite over for holiday dinners, and are the people we can turn to in crisis. That is why they are important. They are family when it counts.

A *replacement* parent is necessary in situations in which there was severe abuse or neglect by early caretakers, and there was no protection. This level of adoption involves a huge commitment on the part of the parent, and a large amount of trust on the part of the person being adopted. One requirement for a *replacement parent* is to be at the *elder* level of maturity, which means the *replacement parent* has already learned a lot about meeting small children's needs, and is ready to help a grown person who is probably stuck at the infant level of maturity. It can be very upsetting for *replacement parents* when they give sacrificially to their infant-level adopt-ees, and get no good feelings in return. In fact, what they often get instead is the adoptee's strong negative, unresolved feelings left over from earlier life. When that happens, the adoptive parents find that their sacrificial giving seems to have backfired! Do not be discouraged. God has redemption in mind, so the sense that "this has backfired" is premature.

Times like this can only turn out right when the *replacement parent* has the maturity and experience to help children achieve their maturity tasks under difficult conditions, and when there is the certainty that this relationship was ordained by God. That certainty is stronger when there are elders who affirm it, and when there are people working together as a caring family and community to overcome the deficits in the adoptee's background.

Here is an important lesson we have learned at Shepherd's House about pain and adoption. People need a joyful identity that is bigger than the traumas they are ready to take on in recovery. Another way to say that is this: People cannot recover from traumas that are bigger than the size of their joyful identity. That being the case, we can understand one way in which spiritual adoption involves pain. When people are adopted, it increases the size of their "joy bucket," so that they can hold more joy, and are now able to deal with more pain. That is good, because it means they are at a point where we can make some headway in recovery, but it will also be pain-ful. Particularly when the adoptee is a person who has infant-level maturity, there will be quite a lot of joyful identity building to be accomplished, and there will also be a lot of pain to be uncovered from the traumas that kept the individual stuck at the infant level of maturity in the first place. Because we have observed this process several times, it seems important to prepare adoptive parents for the fact that they will not be able to remain in touch only with pleasant feelings. Joy will be there, but so will pain. Pain does not mean that something is going wrong with the adoption – it means that God is redeeming the pain in the person's life, which would not have been possible without the adoptive relationship.

Another important lesson that we have learned is that therapists can go through calamitous endings with adoptees who need replacement parents. In cases where the therapist adopts a client at this level of adoption, the client may come to sense that a deep belongingness need can only be met by the therapist. This would be expected to happen when the client did not get those particular needs met during the infant years. Here is the problem: These feelings need to be resolved, in order for the person to move up to higher levels of maturity. Unresolved infant belongingness needs translate into this: "I need you all the time! When I'm not with you I'm empty. When I'm away from you I don't belong." No therapist can solely meet the belongingness needs of any client, in the same way that no single family member can meet the belongingness needs of any young child. It takes a whole family, it takes a *community* of caring men and women, and it takes caring friends. A therapist is not enough. The therapist needs to pay attention to the people in the client's world, so that belongingness needs can be successfully met with those people. The calamity happens when a client persists in turning exclusively to any one person to get belongingness needs met. No single person can meet another person's need to belong. Maturity, belonging, and recovery must all be working together among a group of caring people. Anything else does not fit with the way God designed us.

LESSON

9

BELONGING
Part 1

1. What new insights did you gain from the story about the teenage boy, his struggles and his recovery? Pg 110-111
2. Why is it so important during the teenage years that people have other adults, in addition to their parents, to encourage and develop their identities and their talents? Pg 110-111
3. Describe in your own words what spiritual adoption is, and what it is not. What is your reaction to the concept of spiritual adoption? Pg 111-115
4. If spiritual adoption is building bonds in relationships that God ordains, how does one know when God may intend for someone to adopt or be adopted? Pg 111-115
5. The key experience of adoption is that God's redemption (deliverance, rescue, liberation, recovery) is going on and you are part of it. Have you had this type of relationship before? If so, how did it impact/change you? Pg 113-115
6. Describe what is meant by either receiving or giving life in a spiritual adoption at the stand-in level. Pg 117
7. Describe what is meant by either receiving from a supplemental family member or being a supplemental family member for someone God has brought into your life. Pg 117
8. Do you look to only one or two people to meet your needs? If so, how can you increase your community support, and how can you be someone's support? Pg 119

Anticipating Problems in Spiritual Adoption

A note of caution seems important, concerning people who *volunteer* to become an adoptive family member. Whenever this happens, attention should turn to the readiness of the volunteer. We know of many well-intentioned, would-be spiritual parents who looked at spiritual adoption as though it were a ministry project. Those cases clearly turned out badly for everyone involved. That is *not* how spiritual adoption is supposed to work. Wounded people who need adoption are not projects – they are real people whose needs require sacrificial involvement. Being a spiritual adopting person is about heeding God's direction as *He* brings people together, at just the right time. People are not supposed to stand up and volunteer to adopt people. Whenever God sets things in motion, people can recognize that adoption is underway. Without His direct involvement, there will be frustration and disaster for everyone. We have found that the people who volunteer to adopt, often have deep, unhealed wounds of their own, and are probably not quite mature enough to participate in spiritual adoption.

Here is a truth that underlies spiritual adoption: *Only God can organize and orchestrate spiritual adoption. He plans it, directs it and places people together. We just need to listen to His voice and obey His direction. With God in charge, participating in spiritual adoption is actually participating in God's amazing, transforming redemption!*

A second note of caution is also appropriate. Spiritual adoption can expose powerful feelings that need to be healed, and those powerful feelings can introduce a lot of upset into the life of a family. God seems to work wonders, as He brings redemption while we are adjusting to the emerging family changes. Keep in mind that He is growing us up! He puts us through the transformation cycle, which is mentioned in Chapter 2, and that involves brokenness and repair for the adopters and the adoptees, along the road to maturity. However, it is calming, even in the middle of upsetting moments, to keep in mind that God individually sculpts each situation and each relationship to match the wounds and needs of the individuals involved. Spiritual adoption is always initiated by the Holy Spirit, agreed to and accepted by the people involved, and entered into with a humble heart, and with much fear and trembling.

There is no map or rulebook to follow, but here are some principles to understand:

1. Spiritual adoption is about recognizing brokenness and meeting belongingness needs. Therefore, it requires an honest acknowledgement of the fact that it will take other people to meet those needs.
2. Each adoption is customized by God to meet the needs of the persons involved. If a person's wound was made by a man, there will probably be a man who can play a crucial part of that person's restoration. God will probably not provide a mother to fill a particular need for a person whose wound calls for the availability of a father.

Spiritual adoption is intended to meet the needs of all the people involved. To those who are at the later stages of maturity, it will fulfill their needs to give. For those at the earlier stages, they will benefit from receiving. In this way, a number of people may meet important needs through a single adoption into a family. This is not, and never can be, a case of one person ministering to another out of the abundance of their health and wholeness. In fact, people who venture into these woods should be prepared to face all of their own wounds and neediness! This process is intended by God to be redemptive for all those involved.

Here are a few red flags to keep watching for which signal that spiritual adoption is being misused:

1. Be sure to seek spiritual discernment to determine whether a particular relationship is ordained by God. If it is your idea, or the other person's idea, instead of being orchestrated by God, there will only be trouble ahead.

2. Do not enter an adoptive relationship out of fear. If you have been coerced, frightened or manipulated into making the adoption, it will not work. It needs to be kept in mind that *we should not be looking for people to adopt.* We should be looking at God, so that we can accept whatever He has for us to do.

3. Seek the wisdom of godly people who understand spiritual adoption, who know their hearts, and who know you. If they signal caution or disapproval, the adoption may not be ordained by God.

4. Do not enter an adoption because *you need something* like affirmation, safety, family, relief or companionship. A person should never spiritually adopt in order to get a need met. A person should only adopt because God has set it in motion.

5. Never enter the adoptive relationship to make the adoptee feel better. Spiritual adoption is not an intervention for recovery.

6. Do not think that you are the only person who is available to help someone. This can easily lead to rescuing the person, instead of adopting the person into a welcoming family. The only reason to adopt is because it has been orchestrated by God.

What Spiritual Adoption Looks Like

A man, rejected by his father and wounded in his masculinity, has since childhood yearned for an older brother to "show him the ropes" of becoming a man. He develops a friendship with another man, also wounded, but in different areas. This eventually becomes a mutual brother/brother adoption. They extend themselves to each other in ways they would not do if they were just friends. Their children refer to their father's brother as "uncle." They celebrate birthdays and holidays together. They break all the rules of traditional "friendship" (borrowing money, living together, sharing all their secrets), and none of this hurts the relationship. In fact, these real-life experiences enhance the relationship. They fight and laugh together and stick up for each other the way brothers do. The relationship feels more like family to each of them than any of the relationships they have had with their own biological family members. They learn from each other what it means to be men, and both receive healing for their masculine wounds.

A woman survives a frightening and traumatic childhood where she is molested not just by her father, but also by her brother. In the fullness of time for her redemption, God provides a new father, one who cherishes and nurtures her and wants to keep her safe, and also a brother, who is a friend and an encourager. She learns for the first time that there are two men in the world who care for her, want to be with her, and do not want to use her for sex. She begins to see that men, and even God, can be trusted and enjoyed, and she reaches out to other abused women with a message of hope and redemption.

There are other adoptions that are not as inclusive or complete. A friend rejoices with another friend over the purchase of his first new car, which is something this man's father would have never taken the time to do. He takes him for a ride in it. The friend wants to see the engine and hear the stereo turned up full blast. The man who bought the car receives some "Dad stuff" that will stay with him long after the shiny new car is history. A friend takes another man camping for the first time. He learns how to build a fire and set up a tent. He learns how to develop his resources and talents and to do hard things. More "Dad stuff." This is redemption at work.

A woman finally has a little sister to go shopping with and talk over makeup and new boyfriends – "girl stuff" – that was absent in her family, where she lived with a frightened mother and an abusive father. This is another example of redemption at work through spiritual adoption.

There are countless ways God calls us to provide for each other's needs through spiritual adoption, whether it may be as a *stand-in, supplemental,* or *replacement* family member. What is necessary to participate in spiritual adoption is not skill, degrees in psychology or even emotional health. It is simply a belief in redemption – a conviction that the blessing is stronger than the curse. That is how the family of God becomes mature and complete – one adoption at time.

How this Applies to Ministry

Pastors and Christian leaders at all levels need to see that their calling is ministry, and ministry certainly includes getting involved with people to give them what their hearts need. Regular time needs to be devoted in the family of God for teaching and discussion of these areas: (1) promoting maturity, (2) practicing and teaching the importance of meeting belongingness needs through spiritual adoption, and (3) providing training and opportunities for trauma recovery. Ministry means participating in and sharing people's lives in each of these three areas. If something in a person's life or in the life of a family seems stuck, look for a deficit in each of these areas.

Guidelines to Improve Your Belonging

1. Start by assessing your sense of belonging. Talk things over with members of your family and with key members of your community about what you can do to improve receiving and giving in your relationships with them. Search for specific things that you can do to solve problems in those relationships.

2. Love bonds meet belongingness needs. Find ways to increase sharing and physical closeness, because these are strengtheners for love bonds. Look for specific things to do with the people you love that will produce celebration and enjoyment. Fiercely protect the time that is set aside for these joy-producing activities.

3. Prayerfully consider if there is a person God may be bringing into your life to give you the things that you are lacking, or to fill in a gap in your family.

4. Prayerfully consider if there is a person God may be bringing into your life for you to offer the specific things that they are lacking or to fill in a gap in their family.

5. Invite others who know you and God well to help you identify the characteristics of your heart so that you can increasingly live from the heart Jesus gave you, rather than living from logic, pain or from your own understanding.

6. Look for at least three people "upstream" from you that give you life and three people "downstream" who receive life from you. If you have deficits in either area, pray that these needs would be met through the appropriate spiritual adoptions.

LESSON

10

BELONGING
Part 2

1. What are some of the potential issues/problems that can arise with people who want to volunteer to be up-stream people in spiritual adoption? Pg 121

2. What is your response to the fact that the process of spiritual adoption can bring strong feelings and turmoil for both parties, even though God has individually designed each situation and each relationship to be redemptive for both parties? Pg 121-122

3. Which of the two principles for spiritual adoption do you believe is harder for people to accept and to do? Explain. Pg 122

4. What is your reaction to reading the red flag signals that spiritual adoption is being misused? How might your group or church assist members to avoid falling into these? Pg 122-123

5. Review the different examples of what spiritual adoption can look like. Pg 122-125
    a. Could you benefit from one of these types of adoption? Which one? Would you ask God for it?
    b. Is there one example that you could do for someone else? Do you have the capacity for it now, or is it something to look forward to?

6. Which of the six questions in the "Guidelines to Improve Your Belonging" is the easiest for you to do, and which is the most the difficult? Explain why. Pg 126

CHAPTER

5

YOUR HEART

We all seek direction, especially a spiritual guidance for our life. Let us now look at how we achieve the knowing and discernment to guide our lives wisely. All valid spiritual direction comes to us through our heart – the seat of true knowing and our "eyes and ears" in the spirit. If we discern the "will of God" it is through our heart. Knowing our true identity and destiny is achieved through our heart as well.

Where our eyes look determines what we see. So, when the spiritual eyes of our hearts are turned toward God, we see truth and receive guidance and discernment. This is not hard for us as God's children because joy motivates our hearts to watch God endlessly. Watching God springs from a love-bond with God. Jesus highlighted this truth when He said that wherever our treasure was, there we would find our hearts also (Luke 12:34). Consequently, we are instructed to love the Lord our God with all our heart and strength. Only with our hearts turned to God can we have confidence in what we know. We can see what is good, what we should do, and who we are. If we look away from God, what we will discern (see and hear) is anybody's guess.

True Knowing and False Knowing

If our hearts were all we had, knowing would be simply a matter of where we were looking, but we are greatly burdened by another form of false knowing. Just as the heart is the "organ" of true knowing when turned toward God, we also have an "organ" of false knowing. In the original Greek language of the New Testament, this organ of deceptive knowing is called the *sarx*. We have within us two separate and competing ways to know – the heart which can sometimes be right and true and the sarx which is always wrong and false. The *sarx* is the seat of false discernment, false guidance, and false knowledge of good and evil.

By the *sarx* we mean the human ability to know, judge or perceive good and evil. It is this knowledge of good and evil which we were never intended to have and which is always **false knowing**. No human can correctly distinguish good from evil regardless of their spiritual state, knowledge of scripture, or experience. Our only capacity to form such a judgment comes from the *sarx*, and the *sarx* is always wrong. This seems so simple that it is hard to believe. We should never have had a *sarx*, and we should be in a hurry to get free from its influence.

True knowing seems to be hidden in a great thorny maze of confusion and misconception that stands guard around our think-

ing about the heart and the *sarx*. Even the word *sarx*, translated as
"flesh," "old nature," or "sin nature" inspires so much confusion
and emotion that many people simply stop thinking entirely at the
very mention of the word. Meanwhile, some Bible students assume
that they understand the Greek word *sarx* so quickly that they don't
stop to think it over again. We have decided to use the obscure
spelling *sark* in order to jog their attention.

A similar confusion exists about the heart. When we teach that
our heart is the means of **true knowing** many ask, "Doesn't Jeremiah 17:9 say 'the heart is desperately wicked, who can know
it?'" This verse, they think, means God is warning us to never trust
our hearts. Actually, in this passage God is warning us to keep our
hearts healthy and not trust a sick heart, as we will see in a moment. God wants us to be able to see and hear Him through our
hearts, which is why our heart's health matters. First, our hearts
must be in good health, but then these spiritual "eyes and ears" of
ours must be turned toward God for us to know truth. We must
love God with all our heart according to both Jesus and the Law
of Moses. Jesus Himself comes to dwell specifically in our hearts
(Ephesians 3:17).

The three conditions of **true knowing** are these:

1. Our hearts must be the healthy hearts that Jesus gave us.
2. Our hearts must be turned toward God with all our love and
   strength.
3. We must weed out and avoid the words and judgments of the
   sark.

The three conditions of **false knowing** are these:

1. We are listening to our own understanding (the *sark*).
2. Our hearts are too sick, blind or deaf to discern God.
3. Our hearts are not turned toward God but are loving and
   listening to a different source.

*Trust in the Lord with all your **heart** and lean not on your own understanding (sark); in all your ways acknowledge (discern, know, focus your heart on) Him and He will direct your paths (Proverbs 3:5-6).*

A Healthy Heart

Under the conditions that prevail here on earth our hearts tend to get sickly, dull, hardened or even stone-cold dead. Unfortunately the same is not true of the *sark*, which grows like a weed and threatens to choke out all else. The severest removal of *sark* sprouts is necessary to allow room for the heart to flower and grow. The Old Testament prophets narrate the record of how the people's hearts took sick and died while their *sark* prospered – each one did what was right in their own eyes.

Isaiah gives us the first heart checkup in the year King Uzziah died. He is sent to warn the people that their hearts are "fat" or sick. Their hearts are sluggish so they "hear but don't understand, see but don't perceive." (Isaiah 6: 9-10) They cannot know truth because their hearts can't see or hear anymore.

About 120 years later Jeremiah brings an even worse report. The people's hearts are now incapable of knowing. The text of chapter 17 verse 9, which we quoted earlier, uses the words "sick, sick" to describe their hearts. Using a word twice like that in Hebrew intensifies the meaning of sick. We can render this phrase "deathly ill" or "extremely sick." The King James Bible translated the phrase as "desperately wicked," which is true but somewhat misleading. The point is that a "desperately ill" heart cannot be trusted to discern or know anything.

Thirty years after Jeremiah, the prophet Ezekiel announced that the *sark* infestation was so bad it had killed the people's hearts entirely. They defiled their own land "by their own way" (Ezekiel 36:17), and their hearts were now stone-cold-dead (36:26). Their only hope was to be given a new heart. This is the heart that Jesus gives, a heart like His – where He can live, be seen and heard. The heart that loves God can show us how to act like our true selves.

Living from the heart Jesus gave you means you are being the person you were designed to be. You are acting like yourself. The heart is the place of spiritual discernment where you know who you are. When you are living from your heart, you are following an inner directive that, if governed by the Spirit of God, keeps you on the path that is spiritually attuned to you. You are following God's leading.

Getting to Know the Characteristics of Your Heart

Through our hearts we see ourselves as God sees us. The hearts Jesus gives are like His own, only smaller, with certain characteristics of His in greater quantity than others. In our staff we find one heart is more kind, another long-suffering, a third gives, while another restores. Made in God's image, each heart resonates with God's character, but demonstrates some specific aspects of Jesus' personality more intensely than others. It takes a group of us to demonstrate God's diversity as each one of us reveals a different bit of God's craftsmanship.

Our heart life is the life of the spirit, since it is through our hearts that we know spiritual truth. Spiritual sight from the "heart Jesus gave you" is necessary to discover the unique God-given features we call the "characteristics of your heart." Because the Lord God has handcrafted you for a very specific purpose in His kingdom (Ephesians 2:10), your heart has been fitted to meet that mission. As you live increasingly from your heart, and according to your heart's design, these "characteristics of your heart" will become more evident to you and to others as well. These characteristics of your heart reveal your mission.

One sign that you have found the characteristics of your heart is when your passion, purpose, talents and pain all come together and begin defining who you are. Anne Bierling began finding the characteristics of her heart this way.

One of Anne's greatest passions is to restore. Even as a child she loved restoring beauty from chaos, like cleaning a messy room or organizing an avalanching closet. As a woman, she loves decorating her home by taking "odd and ends" and using them to achieve an aesthetically pleasing interior design.

God has also moved her passion for restoration into other areas like restoring broken people and crumbling marriages – where she achieves a whole other kind of aesthetically pleasing "interior design."

As she grew professionally, Anne was promoted to positions of authority: from assistant principal to membership on a statewide board of directors. In these roles it became apparent that many of her God-given talents had positioned her to be a spokesperson for the truth. Prior to this time, the *sark* had worked hard to convince Anne that "the right thing to do" was to tell the truth only if it were "the nice thing to do." So while her heart kept leading to truth, her *sark* deceptively argued it would not be okay to upset anyone or take the chance that they would dislike her.

As the battle increased, it finally became apparent to Anne that one of the characteristics of her heart was to be a "woman of truth." God had been preparing her for 27 years for that mission. That realization gave Anne both freedom and peace to be the person she was designed to be. She could be true to herself and true to others – making all her endeavors more productive and effective.

When Anne realized her passion for restoration and talents for speaking the truth were intricately knit into a divine purpose, everything suddenly fit together. She could now live truthfully and unapologetically from her heart. She had been crafted to deliver truth: not recklessly and audaciously, but carefully and powerfully, using God's timing and gentle strength. Did it involve pain, risk and fear? Of course. Did it deliver life, freedom and beauty? Oh yes – and it was worth every ounce of sacrifice, sweat and pain that God had used to chisel out in her the true characteristics of her heart.

Getting to know our hearts should not wait until we have grown up. *Children learn to live out of their hearts when they are enjoyed for who they are.* When they are not enjoyed, attended to, or made to feel cherished, it is hard for them to find or appreciate their hearts. Their hearts will be filled with the pain and sadness God also experiences when children are not welcomed. Fortunately, God has made our hearts durable enough that even under extreme abuse and neglect, the characteristics of our hearts are not destroyed, although they may be hidden. People, and particularly children, can have difficulty getting near their hearts when they are in pain. It is hard to listen to our hearts when we hurt.

Sometimes, however, it is our very wounds that put us in touch with the characteristics of our hearts. A boy who grew up neglected and abandoned by his father learned from his own pain to value a father's heart within himself. The wounds in his own soul were transformed by redemption to increase his compassion, love and joy toward his own children. Having suffered himself with abandonment, he did not listen when others told him not to comfort his high-need baby when his own heart insisted on holding the child each night. Although many criticized him, he sensed Jesus smile – through the eyes of his heart. As that baby grew into a confident boy, he saw that his heart had directed him correctly.

The Human Birth Defect

When we were told not to lean on our own understanding, but in all our ways acknowledge God to direct us, there was a reason. Our understanding and reasoning, no matter how informed, are still faulty. Our choice of what is good will always be off. Choosing for ourselves gets in the way of living from our hearts. This problem began in the Garden of Eden. Adam and Eve were instructed not to eat from the tree of the knowledge of good and evil. They neither knew the difference between good and evil nor did they even think about it. Instead, they lived freely and spontaneously out of an inner sense of who the Creator God designed them to be. They lived in an intimate relationship and joyful communication with God who did know the difference between good and evil.

When Adam and Eve set their hearts to listen to the serpent and let him direct their choices, they ate from the tree of the knowledge of good and evil. That moment they gained for us flawed discernment – the *sark*. They began hallucinating that they could see for themselves what was good. From then on every generation has received a "picker" to make us think we can know the difference. This picker thinks it sees the good thing to do, the righteous way to act, and the evil in ourselves and others.

In the Garden of Eden we lost our heart and gained the sark which makes it impossible for us to actually pick the right thing to do. Adam and Eve ushered us into a battle that was never meant for us. We were meant to be oblivious to good and evil, having God direct our paths. Now we all have this human birth defect which Christians are used to thinking of as our "flesh." Christians are used to thinking that the "flesh" (or *sark*) makes us do bad things. Actually, the sark's most harmful effect is that it makes us think we are doing something right and good when we are actually doing or thinking the wrong thing. This happens each time we figure things out on our own instead of following God's direction.

Becoming a Christian and receiving the Holy Spirit does not take away the problem. We still have our *sark* (the flawed picker) so whatever we pick will be wrong. Furthermore, God will not fix or redeem the picker so there is zero chance it will ever be right. This leaves us with the terrifying problem: whenever we try to "figure out" the right thing to do, or "figure out" if something or someone is good, we will always be wrong. Even leaning on our understanding of scripture will not help, for our interpretations are conditioned by the deceit of our *sark*, and limited by our mind. Our wounds and the slanted teachings of our well-intentioned mentors add to the confusion. To use anything we have learned about good and evil to reach our own conclusions, we must activate our *sark* – the only part of us with the audacity and pride to decide on its own what is good and what is evil. The picker is irredeemable. Like a phone book with all the numbers wrong, anything we look up will be incorrect. The *sark* plays spiritual mind games on us and keeps our hearts in a position where they cannot hear the grace-filled directives of our God who wants us to live out of the characteristics He placed within us. We live, or rather die, trying to live from rules and regulations rather than the spirit life within us.

Trying to figure out if something or someone is "good" always plunges us into error. We are always wrong – wrong because we do not see all that God sees. We see and hear what is on the outside while God sees into people's hearts (1 Samuel 16:7). In fact, it is only with long training that the most mature can even begin to sense what God thinks is good and evil (Hebrews 5:14).

We are also wrong about what is "right to do" because our vision falls short of God's ideal. It is our inability to see God's heart perfectly that makes it impossible for us to do things "right." We may be a little bit wrong or 180 degrees off, but nevertheless, we are wrong. Typically, the harder we try to correct things and do things right (the harder we use the *sark*), the farther we get from listening to our heart. The heart discerns spiritual truth but when the *sark* is busy trying to "pick," the mind becomes confused.

We all have that birth defect – our picker. The fight between this birth defect and the heart Jesus gave us never comes to an end during our lifetime.

LESSON

11

HEART
Part 1

1. Describe what you see as the necessary conditions for experiencing valid spiritual direction. Pg 129-130
2. What is your understanding of the sark (the flesh, the old nature, or sin nature) after reading Pg 130-131? What questions do you have, if any?
3. What are the three conditions of "True Knowing?" Which of these is the hardest for you to follow, and why? Which condition of "False Knowing" is hardest for you to get rid of, and why? Pg 131
4. As you read the examples in Anne's story, what personal life events, wounds, passions, etc. came to your mind that can help reveal to you your true heart? What have you learned about your heart from these? Pg 134-135*
5. Describe some of the ways the sark distorts and deceives us into always picking the wrong thing. Pg 136-138
6. "Actually, the sark's most harmful effect is that it makes us think we are doing something right and good when we are actually doing or thinking the wrong thing." What are some examples of this from history and from the Bible ? Pg 136-137
7. What are the steps we can take (our part) to avoid following the "wrong" choices we will make if we listen to the sark?

*An optional interactive assessment of the characteristics of your true heart is available for free at joystartshere.com.

The Heart and the Sark

Religious behavior is what you get when you follow the *sark*. Redemption is what you get when you follow your heart. So what are we to do to get it right? Let's consider the promised gift described in Ezekiel 36: 25-27.

[The Lord says] I will sprinkle clean water on you, and you will be clean; I will cleanse you from all your impurities and from all your idols. I will give you a new heart and put a new spirit in you; I will remove from you your heart of stone and give you a heart of flesh. And I will put my spirit in you and move you to follow my decrees and be careful to keep my laws.

We need to learn from a new reference guide. Our new hearts, not our minds, souls or *sark*, are the place of true knowing. In our hearts we see and hear the Ultimate Guide. Wisdom dictates that our hearts must direct our understanding and knowledge. We follow what we see Jesus doing in our hearts, just as Jesus did what He saw the Father doing. Jesus, our example of one who lived from His heart, constantly watched and listened to God in perfect communion while refusing to pick His own way.

The heart Jesus gives us will tell us what God wants from us even though we cannot always explain it to someone else – and maybe not even to ourselves. Just like a young daughter knows what Mommy wants her to do but cannot prove that what Mommy wants is good, so the heart knows what God wants, even though we cannot prove to our *sark* that it is good. What God wants is good, even though our picker's evaluation does not justify what our heart is saying. According to the *sark*, the expensive perfume poured on Jesus should have been sold and the money given to the poor. Mary should have worked as hard as Martha. To this day, even those who decry legalism in the church are prone to think they can figure out the "right way" for themselves and others to behave. This is not possible.

The evaluations of others or even the guilt and praise produced by our own *sark* must not decide for us whether we have done what is good or right. Ironically, those who have the greatest difficulty accepting that they are without the ability to decide what is good or evil, are the religious people of the world. Although Jesus only did what He saw His Father doing, Jesus was constantly seen as "bad" by the religious leaders. During a confrontation with them, described in Mark 7, Jesus was berated by the Pharisees for not doing what was right and holy. (The teachers of the law made this call courtesy of their knowledge of good and evil – the *sark*.) Jesus responded strongly with a text from Isaiah.

These people honor me with their lips, but their hearts are far from me. They worship me in vain; their teachings are but rules taught by men. You have let go of the commands of God and are holding on to the traditions of men. And he said to them, "You have a fine way of setting aside the commands of God in order to observe your own traditions!"

In Matthew 23 we read how Jesus described the sarx-driven lives of the best Bible quoting "pickers" of His day. These Scribes and Pharisees, meticulously copied the word of God by hand and made a life of studying it. Jesus said their recommendations of "the right thing to do," bound heavy burdens on others, were self-serving and wounded the weak. He said in verses 23-24: "Woe to you, teachers of the law . . . you have neglected the more important matters of the law – justice, mercy and faithfulness. . . . You blind guides!"

When we listen to our *sark*, we fail to hear what God is doing in the lives of others. The *sark* also blinds us to God's activity in us. Jim Wilder began to discover the struggle between his heart and *sark* one cold December as he listened to a pastor's wife tell about leaving her abusive husband. Moving out immediately meant she could not provide gifts or even a Christmas meal for her two young daughters. She tried to be brave and comfort herself with the thought that at least her husband could no longer molest the girls. Jim's heart told him it was unkind to let the three go without a Christmas dinner. His *sark* said it would be a boundary violation to give her food, gifts or money. But the kindness Jesus placed in his heart proved too strong, so he bought everything the mother needed to have a good Christmas meal and meals for the rest of the month as well. Jim's *sarx* was not done with him though, and it convinced him to lie to the mother about the source of the food. He claimed some church had dropped it off – this way he could appear to not violate any boundaries. Jim had listened to his heart and they were blessed, but his *sarx* was still alive and bothering him.

The *sark* persistently tries to destroy the heart. The apostle Paul described this well in Romans, chapters seven and eight. Those who live according to the *sark* die, but those who live by the Spirit find life and peace.

Winning Battles With Your Sark

The sark is the mortal enemy of your heart. Since the heart is where we achieve **true knowing**, it should come as no surprise that the heart's mortal enemy tells lies – the most useful lie of all being the claim that the *sark* is telling the truth about what is really good for us. **False knowing** makes us vulnerable to other sources of lies.

The *sark* soon finds itself making common cause with cultural lies (from the world) and spiritual lies (from evil supernaturalism). This false knowing can only be combated by a return to hearts that love God with all their strength in concert with their souls and minds.

In day-to-day existence, the *sark* has two ways of blocking our hearts – the *sark's* opinion at the moment, and the accumulated effect of all the **false knowing** in our life until now. These lies, imbedded in our experience, are much harder to catch than the logical-sounding lies the *sark* tells moment by moment. It would actually be very hard to locate this experiential base of false knowing except that lies always leave a trail of unresolved painful feelings. Wherever there is unresolved pain left by traumas, you can be sure the sark left the lies of **false knowing** imbedded in your memory. These lies, called experiential lies, are the *sark's* opinion about what happened, what it meant, and what was good or evil.

Trauma produces lasting pain through **experiential lies** left by the sark or its two friends – cultural lies and deceptive spirits. These deceptions about what is good or evil about us or our world are blended into painful experiences and left to fester in our memories. Since our responses in life are directed by our experience, these experiential lies will then direct our actions, feelings, views, relationships, choices and values in ways we no longer even think about.

A little girl is molested. In her pain and confusion the *sark* concludes, "This happened to you because you are bad." A cultural lie says she was acting seductively. A fallen angel says, "You will never be clean." Unremoved, these lies will continue causing pain, destroying her life, and disconnecting her from her heart.

The *sark* seems to dig its roots into all our soul's unresolved pain, and there gain the energy to grow vigorously. From our suffering the sark produces reasonable sounding **logical lies** about what is good and evil. Whatever hurts us is evil and whatever would save us from pain is good. "Jesus doesn't love me because He didn't save me from being hurt," is one example. These *sark*-picked versions of good and evil are the lies we love to hear because they justify our beliefs about our pain. Wounded people often have trouble listening to their hearts because their *sark* is so loud and strong.

As we invite Jesus, the one who lives in our heart, into our unresolved pain we **experience** the truth about ourselves and others. This healing and change takes place in our hearts. Through our heart's **true knowing** we expose and demolish all the experiential lies hidden in our painful memories. We come to know the truth about ourselves, our histories and others through the eyes of our heart. This is why Jesus says we must forgive others "from our heart" (Matthew 18:35).

People who have been healed by a personal experience of Jesus entering their painful memories report freedom, no more need to judge those involved, and most profoundly, a **knowing** that what they now see about themselves and the situation is unquestionably, profoundly and peacefully true. **True knowing** comes to the heart that sees and hears "God with us."

Common examples of this change come from people who cried out to Jesus for help while they were being assaulted or abused, but God did not stop the assault. One man, whose *sark* concluded that Jesus liked the abuse, brought Jesus to this memory and asked the Lord if what his *sark* said was true. He saw Jesus weep with him and he was comforted. The woman whose *sark* concluded, "Jesus is too weak to help me," heard Him say, "Someday you will understand." For her, this brought peace. The girl who believed, "I am too evil to save," found herself lifted from the darkness and dressed in white. Each one who searched for truth in their heart received a simple answer that brought peace. They knew the answer was truth. They had seen and heard God. They needed nothing else.

As for the logical sounding lies of the *sark*, we must reject them with vigor like we would pull a weed. Again the answer lies in knowing the truth. We bring to God what the sark has said and ask in our heart, "Is that true?" God's answer to our hearts sets us free.

Maribeth Poole ended her schooldays by running to the top step of the girl's dorm where she wept alone. She was only five years old and away at boarding school, far from any comfort. Maribeth did this every day for weeks until one day when she arrived, she found another little girl had gotten there first and was already crying. Since her place had been taken, Maribeth sat down next to the other little girl and comforted her and never cried again. The house-parents concluded that since Maribeth no longer showed any needs, she was now mature. This implanted a cultural lie that not having needs makes one mature.

From her feelings of hopelessness her sark concluded another false "*truth*" – other people mattered, but Maribeth did not. Her experience made her believe that if Jesus had come to be with the girls on that step, He would have comforted the other girl and ignored Maribeth. The pain of this false knowing continued to intrude into her adult life reducing her ability to express need and her capacity to know her heart.

Years later, as a counselor, Maribeth began discovering her heart. She felt drawn to comfort clients whose suffering did not stop between sessions. When she made contact with clients in their real life outside the office, the rest of the counseling staff where she worked at that time advised her that such a personal expression was unprofessional – a bad thing to do. Staff meetings soon polarized. The staff were certain they could pick the right thing to do, while Maribeth was unable to justify why her heart said differently. The staff wanted her to fear-bond with them about being sued, while Maribeth's heart wanted to love-bond with hurting people. Meanwhile she had to battle her own *sark's* message that other people's needs should be met while hers should be overlooked. It was in her heart that Jesus spoke truth to both cultural and sark lies. Only in her heart did she find that God loved them all – Maribeth, the clients and the staff.

You Will Know Your Heart

1. When your heart is healthy and alive.
2. When you turn your heart toward God with all your love and strength.
3. When you let your pain tell you what really matters to your heart and hear what God says about your hurt.
4. When you are receiving and giving life in your important relationships.
5. Whenever you act like your true self.
6. Whenever you resist the *sark*.
7. When those who know their heart tell you what they see in yours.

Living From Your Heart

Living from the heart Jesus gave you means you are being the person you were designed to be, acting like yourself in all situations. This can be an illusive concept at first. Let us give another example from our own lives.

Rick Koepcke and his wife had two beautiful children who were well-behaved and easy to love. They also had careers they liked, a good marriage, and good friends. They seemed to be doing everything "right." People told them God would surely bless them because they were living "right."

God did something for them alright! He began messing up their lives by bringing some very broken people to them. Rick, who had a father's heart, felt God's call to spiritually adopt some of these broken people and bring them into his nice little family. He started inviting them to family events, and having birthday parties for them. His behavior didn't fit any "rules" he knew about. He was following what his heart told him to do. This caused pain and conflict within his marriage, forcing him and his wife to look at their own wounds more closely. The willingness to go through pain and difficulty for these broken children taught Rick that the characteristics of his heart included compassion. Being a man of compassion and integrity, who was willing to fight for all of his children, brought Rick joy and showed others the characteristics of his heart. As his family moved from upheaval to pain and back to joy, they discovered that God was redeeming not just these broken people they were adopting, but their lives as well. His children got a bigger picture of God's heart and expanded their definition of "family."

Living from the heart does not mean we throw away all the rules and live by our "feelings." The heart is much deeper than our emotions. The heart that Jesus gives is the most solid thing about us. Often our emotions become overwhelmed when our soul is unable to bear all that the heart knows, but as our joy-strength increases we learn to live with our hearts.[5]

When we look into God's face with the eyes of the heart Jesus gave us, He makes His face shine upon us with joy. God is "glad to be with us" no matter the state we are in – whether in shame, anger, fear, disgust, humiliation or even hopeless despair. We love Him for it, and He teaches us how to act like ourselves so we, in turn, can be with each other and bring each other back to joy, build love bonds, and comfort one another with the comfort we have received.

---

[5]   If you wish to delve more deeply into developing a God-directed life, read *The Divine Conspiracy*, by Dr. Dallas Willard.

LESSON

12

HEART
Part 2

1. The gospels record how the sark-driven religious leaders repeatedly confronted and criticized Jesus as He was "doing what He saw his Father doing." How does His example encourage and strengthen Christians as we listen to our hearts and our Father? Pg 140-141

2. What experience have you had that was similar to Jim Wilder's story? When have you completely obeyed the voice of your Father even when others were critical of you? Pg 142

3. What are the two ways that the sark can block our hearts from hearing the true voice of our Father? Pg 143

4. What is your understanding of the interplay of experiential lies, cultural lies and deceptive spirits and how they interact to produce lasting pain that the sark digs its roots into? Pg 143

5. How would you define experiential lies and logical lies? What is your understanding about what is needed to remove each of these? Pg 143-145

6. Maribeth Poole learned lies about herself as a young girl. Where did she find her source of strength, and how did it change her? What freed her from those lies? Pg 145-146

7. Look at the items listed under "You Will Know Your Heart." Which ones are you doing pretty well with, and which ones need more work? Pg 146

6

LIVING
THE LIFE MODEL

We would be amiss if we gave you only pieces of information but no picture of *The Life Model*. Just as every person has a unique, God-given heart, so does every church. When a church discovers its God-given heart, its ministry usually grows and flourishes, and takes on a very personal tone. Interestingly enough, no matter what unique "personality" your church has been given, we believe that *The Life Model* components will be fundamental to the spiritual health and growth of your church body. Here is a universal picture of what we believe any church would look like if its members were living *The Life Model*.

What a Church Looks Like Under The Life Model

This church is led by the Holy Spirit into God's redemptive works. Members look to God for salvation, healing, deliverance from evil, and adoption into the family of God, while seeking after God with all their hearts, minds, and souls. They take seriously the biblical mandates to grow all members to maturity, and this is apparent through the structure of the whole community. Since an understanding of and a commitment to maturity are critical elements we often find missing in the church, this design will focus on the role of maturity in a community without forgetting that it is just one aspect of the church.

Life Model church leaders have all reached at least an adult level of maturity. They know that their actions, both public and private, have an impact on history. The leaders are not focused on recognition, personal "fairness," or popular opinion, but rather on doing what is best for the community and by addressing the truth – even when it requires doing hard things. The leaders understand that people have different levels of maturity, and that someone's biological age may not match his or her maturity age. Leaders not only know how to assess their own and others' maturity levels, but they also understand the tasks required to mature, both in applying it to themselves and in teaching it to others. They use this information wisely to help everyone mature.

Leaders realize that the two types of traumas – the Absence of necessary love and care (Type A traumas) and Bad things that should not happen (Type B traumas) – interfere with the normal process of maturation and that traumas can produce dividedness. They know that unchecked sin and pride can also be great barriers to maturity. Therefore, they have built and modeled a community where individuals can honestly admit their pain and sufferings and receive support and guidance for healing and growth.

The community is careful about whom they place in leadership. They also pray for and work to cultivate maturity in all their members. They know that people who look like an adult may not have even passed the child level of maturity. A pastor is removed after the leaders recognize a child level of maturity. He has not learned to care for himself appropriately and, therefore, struggles to give appropriate care to the youth. He is divided – a part of him does not want God to lead his life. He is put under the care of an elder to bring him to an adult level of maturity so that he can continue using his gifts and talents. Others, who are trained and Spirit-led, are asked to pray and minister healing and integration to him for his dividedness.

Because the community believes that God can truly "take all things and work them for good," the community prays for and fosters *redemption* in all its individuals, desiring every injury or sin (past or present, and sometimes multi-generational) to be redeemed. They pray specifically for *deliverance from evil*, so that the assaults in and around a person's life are stopped. They pray for and promote healing by restoring individuals' capacities to receive and give life, so that no part of them is divided or disconnected from God. And they also pray for and participate in *spiritual adoption* so that new believers and older saints, and wounded hearts and strong families, are all attached by God into spiritual families where they can all mature and flourish.

The community understands that the capacity for joy is fundamental to human growth. Those who have this capacity understand both the importance of building joy in others and of teaching others how to return to joy from every difficult experience or emotion.

Leaders know that the challenge of marriage is only manageable for someone who can take care of self *and* others simultaneously – someone at least at the adult level of maturity. Those with infant or child levels will do poorly in marriage and even worse as parents.

In fact, by understanding the five maturity levels and their necessary tasks, leaders are better able to anticipate and prevent unnecessary crises through solid pre-engagement counseling; while also being able to guide and grow those in the midst of marital turmoil.

The community encourages parents to cherish their children. Parents of infants, children and adolescents limit their involvement in outside duties and activities, realizing that their primary job is the maturing and enjoying of their own children and spouses. These parents know that they are giving without expecting to receive in return. They understand how children develop and what they need in order to mature, and they draw on God's wisdom and upon the wisdom of more mature parents who have already raised children to adulthood to guide their parenting decisions and actions. Parents also understand that in order to "train up a child in the way he should go," they need to work hard to know each of their children individually and assist their children in discovering the unique, God-given characteristics of their hearts.

The community rejoices over children becoming adults. Rites of passage are held for those who have moved from the child level of maturity to the adult level. These individuals have developed their resources and talents, learned to do hard things, begun to accept necessary pain and discovered what is truly satisfying. They have received an understanding of their family history and the history of God's family along with the "big picture" of what life is all about. They know what is expected of them as adults and are prepared for challenges and difficulties because the community has led and assisted them.

Children raised in this church were first introduced into the care of the community at age four or five, when they left infancy/toddlerhood behind. Until then, the focus of every effort was in building strong, loving bonds with their mothers and fathers. Their important needs were met for them until they could learn to identify their own needs and ask for what they needed themselves. At four or five they were ready to take their self-care skills into the community under their parents' watchful care – just as Abraham held a feast at Isaac's weaning so that the community might celebrate and accept his son, who could now feed himself.

The elders have sensed God's leading to oversee the care of other people (especially those without families) in much the same way they care for their own, grown, biological children. Family ties are extended in the spiritual family. The elders care for, protect, love and teach the people that God has given them in later life. They watch with joy as those under their care are increasingly able to receive and give life. They understand that everyone, even (especially) the leaders, need people upstream from them – people who can give them guidance and wisdom as well as love and care.

Leaders know that it is not only the fainthearted and the weak who need adoption. The scriptures cite that Paul had Ruffus' mother "as a mother for himself also" (Romans 16:13). Jesus also completed an adoption on the cross, giving His mother Mary and His beloved disciple John to each other. Many people, who are perceived as strong, benefit enormously from spiritual adoption. It has become clear, that responding to God's voice as He orchestrates spiritual adoption in the church, means the difference between life and death for its members and between revival and decline for the church. People understand that listening to God's call to spiritually adopt can be extremely painful, but also amazingly beautiful, transforming and Christ-like. It requires the guidance of God, the maturity of self, and support from others.

As maturity increases, judging thoughts subside and that hallmark is evident in all the elders of this community. They have the wisdom to identify people's needs and to help them grow. Their leadership is marked by grace, love and sacrifice, not by domination, superiority and judgment. The elders understand the freedom of living from the heart Jesus gave them, and the insidious danger of being ruled by the *sark*. They have also noticed that when they live from their hearts, God's voice becomes clearer. Because these elders have discovered their own unique identities in Christ, they have a God-given ability to help others find, liberate and nurture the characteristics of their own hearts, too.

This community-wide way of living positions everyone to come into a full understanding of our Lord Jesus Christ, and to live from the power of the persons God created them all to be. It is in communities like this that people can gain a sense of belonging that will last for a whole lifetime. Belonging to such a community enlarges people's joyful identity enough so that they can honestly face their traumas, and thereby overcome the life-long barriers that prevent them from reaching their God-given destinies. This is about everyone living from the heart Jesus gave them, and that is truly a very satisfying way to live!

Living in the Family of God

At the beginning of this book, we identified that we were writing to church leaders and to the wounded people in the church community. While those two groups may have seemed strangely incompatible on page 1, our hope is that by now you will have come to see those groups as very similar, both in their needs and in their potentials.

People who are wounded *and* people who lead all need loving families; caring people to help them mature; safe places to honestly share and to heal their personal traumas; and relationships that give them a chance to receive and give life. Furthermore, sometimes leaders become wounded and those who have been wounded develop into mature leaders. For example, a leader may be broadsided by a new trauma or by an old, unresolved wound and need a place to heal, while a wounded person who has been healed, may become a key contributor to the church community. At some point every leader will be in a position to receive life from others, and every wounded person will eventually be in a position to give life to others. We are all designed by God to live life to the fullest when we take part in both ends of the receiving and giving life exchange. Through this process the church comes alive, and everyone realizes that they are a vital part of it!

That is the beauty of the church when it *lives* as the family of God. That is the power of the Christian community when people *live from their hearts*. That is the purpose and power of *The Life Model*.

LESSON

13

LIVING THE LIFE MODEL
Part 1

1. Has your church discovered its unique God-given heart and mission? If so, what would you say it is? Pg 149
2. What has been your experience with how churches have typically tried to mature their members? In what ways is this similar to the Life Model concepts? How is it different from the Life Model? Pg 150
3. Do you think most church leaders understand the different levels of maturity? Why or why not? Pg 150-151
4. Describe the advantages to a church if all the leaders are at adult maturity or higher. Pg 150-151
5. In what ways does your church offer "belonging" to everyone who regularly attends? Are there other ways to do this that you might introduce to your church family? Pg 151-154
6. In what ways does your church help children and adolescents develop their maturity tasks? Are there other ways to do this that you might introduce to your church family? Pg 152-153
7. What are some examples of how the people in your church give life to each other and receive life from one another? Are there other ways to do this that you might introduce to your church family?
8. Describe how the strong (our church leaders) and the weak (the wounded and less mature) people in our churches are similar in both their needs and their potentials. Pg 154-155

LESSON

14

LIVING THE LIFE MODEL
Part 2

"Take a Look At Where You Are" (Pg 159) is an assessment tool to assist you in recording where you are and what growth you have made during this study. It will also assist you in getting a clearer picture of what your next growth steps will be. After you have written your answers to assessment questions, also answer the following questions:

1. How satisfied you are with the way you rated yourself? Explain your answer.
2. How have you seen yourself grow during this study? Give examples.
3. What are one or two goals you have for yourself to continue with your growth now that the study is over?
4. What help do you need to really achieve these goals?
5. Who can you ask to walk with you and support you as you move forward with these maturity goals?

Take A Look At Where You Are

1. MATURITY: Are you reaching your potential?
Examine the first column in the *Maturity Indicators* chart (pages 53-57) and determine your stage of maturity. Which maturity tasks have you completed?

Look at the last column and find which tasks you have failed. What do you need to make up those deficits?

How satisfied are you with your level of maturity?
1 (low) 2 (below average) 3 (average) 4 (above average) 5 (high)

2. RECOVERY: Are you facing the pain in your life and growing?
What Type A and Type B Traumas have you suffered?
What emotions do you get stuck in?
What lies may be hindering your recovery?

How satisfied are you with your recovery?
1 (low) 2 (below average) 3 (average) 4 (above average) 5 (high)

3. BELONGING: Are your relationships driven more by joy or fear?
Do your relationships have "receiving and giving" in them?
Do you have a "family" that knows you and affirms you?
Do you belong to a larger family, like a community, where you
    can receive "elder level wisdom" when you need it?

How satisfied are you with your sense of belonging?
1 (low) 2 (below average) 3 (average) 4 (above average) 5 (high)

4. YOUR HEART: Are you winning the ongoing battle with your sark?
Can you tell when your sark is tugging at you?
Do you have weapons that are effective against the sark?
Is it important for you to seek God's direction?
Do you know the characteristics of your heart?

How satisfied are you with your success in living from your heart?
1 (low) 2 (below average) 3 (average) 4 (above average) 5 (high)

Biblical Underpinnings For The Life Model

MATURITY

Verses where the concept of maturity is significant:
Psalm 148:12; Genesis 44:20; Leviticus 19:32; Proverbs 17:6;
Proverbs 20:29; Joel 2:28; Acts 2:17; I John 2:13-14.

Significant passages where the word for maturity is used:
Luke 2:52; Ephesians 4:11-16; II Peter 1:5-9; II Peter 3:18;
I Corinthians 13:11.

Verses where immaturity is viewed as a problem:
I Corinthians 3:2; Hebrews 5:12-13.

SPIRITUAL ADOPTION

Passages where spiritual family is illustrated:

I Samuel 3:6, 3:16	Eli and Samuel (father – son)
II Samuel 1:26	David and Jonathan (brother – brother)
Mark 10:30	brothers, sisters, mothers, children
John 19:25-27	John and Mary (mother – son)
Romans 16:13	Paul and Rufus' mother (mother – son)
I Corinthians 4:15	(father – children)
I Corinthians 16:12	(brother – brother)
I Timothy 2:1	(father – son)
I Timothy 5:2	(brother – sister, mother – son)
Titus 1:4	(father – son)
Philemon 1:10	Onesimus and Paul (father – son)
I Peter 5:13	Peter and Mark (father/elder – son)

Supplemental Readings

Friesen, James G. *More than Survivors: Conversations with Multiple Personality Clients.* Wipf & Stock Publishers: Eugene, OR, 1992, 1997.

Friesen, James G. *Uncovering the Mystery of MPD.* Wipf & Stock Publishers: Eugene, OR, 1991, 1997.

Wilder, E. James, Coursey, Christopher M., *Share Immanuel: The Healing Lifesyle,* Shepherd's House, East Peoria, IL, 2010.

Wilder, E. James, Khouri, Edward M., Coursey, Christopher M., Sutton, Shelia D., *Joy Starts Here*, Shepherd's House, East Peoria, IL, 2013.

Wilder, E. James. *The Red Dragon Cast Down.* Chosen Books: Grand Rapids, MI, 1999.

Wilder, E. James. *The Complete Guide to Living With Men.* Shepherd's House: Pasadena, CA, 2004.

Willard, Dallas. *The Divine Conspiracy: Rediscovering Our Hidden Life in God.* Harper: San Francisco, CA, 1998.

Appendix A

This text was written by the original authors and placed at the beginning of Chapter 2 in front of the discussion on maturity. Changing fear bonds to love bonds is closely tied to maturity levels and skills so the topic is now after the discussion of maturity levels, but still in Chapter 2. In this edition, the editors have selected an expanded instruction for changing fear to love from Dr. Wilder for the Chapter 2 text, and placed the original text here in Appendix A for the reader.

Changing Fear Bonds Into Love Bonds

One way that you can tell you are in a love-bonded relationship is by the way you feel after you have been with that person. If you generally feel content, energized, secure and confident after being together, it is very likely you have a love bond. Love bonds tend to empower and bring out the best in us. If, however, you typically feel anxious, tense, confused or drained after being with that person, chances are that the relationship is based on fear bonds.

Although difficult, it is possible to turn fear bonds into love bonds. When you can successfully do that, both people have a much greater chance of experiencing joy and returning to joy in the relationship. To make the essential shift, you first need to be able to answer two important questions about yourself:

1. Do I know myself, and what it is like to act like my true self?
2. Can I maintain my sense of self in this relationship?

Steps in making the shift from fear bonds to love bonds.

1. Know and enjoy who you are.
A love-bond based relationship requires two individuals who know their true selves. Therefore, it is vital to know and enjoy the important aspects of who you are before you can fully bond with others. For instance, what brings you great satisfaction? What personal attributes are you most proud of? What helps you experience joy? Can you return to joy from upset feelings without acting in a way you later regret? Do you feel you need prestige or possessions in order to

be liked by others? Are your current relationships characterized by love and freedom or by neediness and fear? Can you be yourself in your relationships? Do you allow other people to be who they are in your relationships?

As you honestly work through these questions and allow more of the person you are to be present in your relationships, you will experience some fear and resistance. Remember, though, that all of us are initially uncomfortable with change. If you have the faith and courage to persevere, you will enjoy yourself more and increase the chance of love bonding with others.

2. *Take responsibility for your own actions and feelings.*
In fear bonds, people often believe they have to guess what the other person is thinking or feeling, and then anticipate how not to upset them. Even if we *could* read other people's thoughts, we could not control how they would react to us, nor is that our responsibility. We are responsible for our own actions. That is all we can control. We are adding fear to the relationship when we control or manipulate or shut down so that the *other person* has to guess what we are thinking or feeling. By taking responsibility for ourselves, but not controlling others, we send a message to them that we are not operating out of fear or desperation – and they do not need to either.

3. *Recognize the fear bonds present in your relationships.*
We are often not aware of the fears that motivate us in a relationship. Typically, fear bonds revolve around these fears:
> a) Fear of rejection. "I have to do everything I possibly can to make this relationship survive."
> b) Fear of anger. "I can't stand having anyone angry at me."
> c) Fear of being shamed. "I can't let anyone see my weaknesses or faults."

4. *Let go of controlling the results.*
Because love bonds are based on your ability to return to joy, they are not dependent on the other's responses or behaviors. Rather, they are based on being yourself in all situations and knowing you are someone enjoyable. Interestingly enough, once you let go of both the need to control relationships and the responsibility for someone else's behaviors and simply concentrate on being yourself, you are more likely to see the results you were hoping for.

Appendix B

What is the Life Model?

So hurt people wouldn't spend their lives simply recovering and "getting by," a small but dedicated group of pastors, counselors, prayer ministers, deliverance workers, abuse survivors, support people, prayer team members, lay leaders, people in recovery and and parents looked, studied and prayed their way to a model that would guide us from birth to death—a LIFE model. The theory behind this book was developed at Shepherd's House Inc. with an international advisory panel from many traditions and theoretical perspectives working together to formulate this profoundly Christian view of life.

The Life Model synthesizes these perspectives into an understandable model. It gives practical guidance on how to maximize each stage of your life, as well as how to minimize the blocks that would keep you from living life to the fullest.

What makes the Life Model a Christian model is a division between redemption and maturity. While most people will agree that not everyone matures correctly, some would say that all human beings could reach their full maturity by purely human means. Christians would say, "not without help." Some believe that everything needed for full human maturity is already contained within each person. Christians would say, "Something is still missing." It takes a mutual effort between people and their God to fully live and experience life as it was meant to be lived. God clearly separates divine areas of responsibility from human areas of responsibility. Humans are responsible for maturity. God is responsible for redemption.

The Life Model is not just a theory – it is a model. The Life Model does not just talk about growing – it gives you practical steps on how to mature. The Life Model does not just promote recovery – it identifies specific ways to heal traumas. The Life Model challenges you to change and grow and be the person that God designed you to be.

The Life Model is an idealized model, that is to say, it proposes what life should be like rather than describing what life on earth generally produces. The Life Model suggests that people need five things in order to thrive:

1. A place to belong
2. To both receive and give life
3. The capacity to recover from malfunctions
4. Maturation
5. To stay true to their identities (hearts)

These five elements develop when we share joy and sorrows together as natural and spiritual families in peaceful homes. The Life Model covers both our growth and recovery. These five elements apply, whether we consider physical growth, emotional growth, family growth, community growth or spiritual growth. Taken in order from one to five, these elements are needed for strong and healthy human growth. Taken in reverse order, starting with living from our true identities, these same elements form an excellent diagnostic grid for a failure to thrive. By understanding the causes for failures to thrive we can design a restoration process.

The Life Model explains how to restore our identities as individuals, families and communities so that we live from a completely synchronized and authentic identity we call "the heart that Jesus gives us." This authentic identity is as much communal as it is individual. Deep in the right hemisphere of every human brain is a control center that develops during the first two years after conception. This center will run our lives and bodies and, provided we develop a strong one, will see us through the tempests of life. We seek to train and restore this control center. With it we can regulate our emotions, act like ourselves and stay synchronized inside and out.

We become traumatized when the emotional intensity of life exceeds our capacity to maintain synchronization between the four levels of our control center. Thriving means building a strong control center through joyful attachment bonds that bring peace and return us to joy when we become upset.

We develop our identities by responding and resonating to the characteristics we possess as we watch them expressed by an older and more experienced person. Identity is propagated like cuttings from live plants, and not grown from seeds. This way of growing an identity by receiving the life passed on from one who went before is true for us at a physical level, just as it is at an emotional and spiritual level.

The Life Model is a profoundly Christian blueprint for wholeness for individuals, families, churches and communities across the lifespan. The Life Model is a unifying approach to ministries of counseling, recovery, pastoral care, prayer ministry, deliverance, inner healing, child rearing, community development, body life and health. The Life Model is used internationally for substance abuse recovery programs, trauma treatment and Christian missions. Missions have adopted the model for the restoration of missionary children. Major ministries that deal with trauma and abuse victims use and distribute the Life Model as part of their teaching. A growing number of books, tapes, videos, conferences and training programs use aspects of the Life Model, as you can see in Appendix D.

Appendix C

The Theoretical Basis for the Life Model

Modified from *The Complete Guide to Living With Men*
© 2003 E. James Wilder

The Life Model

The LIFE Model is, as its name implies, a model for life, from conception to death. It is an idealized model, that is to say, it proposes what life should be like, as opposed to merely describing what life on earth generally produces. In short, the LIFE model proposes that in order to thrive people need five things:
1. A place to belong
2. To both receive and give life
3. The capacity to recover from malfunctions
4. Maturation
5. To stay true to their identities

Research And Resources On Human Development

Many astute observers have given detailed descriptions of child development, particularly mental and verbal abilities. The last few years have produced a new level of observation. Several types of brain scans can now study actual brain activity and discover when and how the brain itself develops. Surgical studies have even studied individual brain cells--discovering such quaint things as brain cells that recognize and respond to facial expressions. Five theoreticians have strongly influenced our knowledge of the link between brain development and the growth of an identity.

Dr. Allan Schore, from the UCLA School of Medicine, has carefully described the many studies on development of the infant brain as it relates to the development of identity. In particular, he has studied the development of the orbital prefrontal cortex. It is called "orbital" because it sits right behind the socket (orbit) of the eyes. This is the part of the brain that is at the top of the command hierarchy and is connected to every major system in the body--even the immune system. It is the first part of the cortex to receive information from inside the body or outside as well. Dr. Schore's work is notable in describing how this part of the brain (which we have called the "joyful identity control center") develops and works.

Dr. Schore has written some of the best technical descriptions of current research on brain changes during the development of maturity. He has combined the theories and discoveries of three different disciplines in order to make sense of very complex and separate fields.

Summary of Bonding Development and the Senses

0 - 1.5 months	Taste, smell and temperature
1.5 - 3 months	Touch
3 - 12 months	Visual (facial expressions of emotion)
12 - 24 months	Auditory (voice tone)

Dr. Schore's brain model is hierarchical, which is a very important distinction from others we studied. His diagram entitled *Schore's Right Brain Dual Corticolimbic-Autonomic Circuits* outlines the ascending levels of the brain's emotional control center. This hierarchy is particularly significant because it explains why trouble at a lower lever will affect all the levels above it. Schore's hierarchical three-level structure is the basis for the four level control structure in the right hemisphere used in the Life Model. The top three levels of my model, the prefrontal cortex (4), cingulate cortex (3), and the amygdala (2) are directly from Dr. Schore's theory. The bottom layer (related to attachment) is suggested by the work of Dr. Siegel and the brain scans by Dr. Amen, whose work we will examine in a moment.

There are three distinctive elements to Dr. Schore's theories that, when combined, make his theories stand out above the others. First is his understanding that brain structures function in a hierarchical way rather than a modular one. Second, his model is based on synchronization of brain activation in time "windows," not just brain area functions or biological states. Third, Dr. Schore's brain model is both individual and mutual--subjective and inter-subjective. What we can make of this is a brain where small critical areas make great differences to the rest of the brain. The overall performance of the brain is not simply a matter of what its parts can do, but what they do together at a given moment in time. And our brains are not so private and locked in our skulls as we might suspect, but rather share powerful, mutual states of mind at given moments in time with other brains. These states are so closely linked that we can conceive of both an individual and a mutual mind, which must both be running well across the entire lifespan. We will return to this discussion in a moment after we examine other contributors.

Dr. Erik Erikson of Harvard was unusual in that he developed a model of human growth that did not stop with childhood, but continued across the lifespan. Erikson's eight crises provide us with a useful description of development. Although he was not involved in brain growth studies, later research has found that some of Erikson's crises represent a switch in development from one side of the brain to the other. The first crisis represents right hemisphere growth, the second is left hemisphere and the third is right hemisphere. The connections between what he observed and brain development in infancy have greatly expanded as new methods and technology have been developed. The massive amounts of current knowledge have been collected and summarized by three researchers in particular—Dr. Schore, Dr. van der Kolk and Dr. Siegel.

Dr. Bessel van der Kolk, from Boston University School of Medicine and Harvard University, has done in-depth study in the area of trauma and deprivation. Dr. van der Kolk has written summaries of early bonding research and added his own studies on the effects of early traumas at different ages. From this work we can see the tremendous deficits caused by early psychological injuries and deprivations. He details the neurotransmitter, immune system, biochemical, developmental, and social impacts of early deprivation, loss and trauma. He points out that there are critical periods for attachment and brain growth. Early trauma results in a life-long inability to regulate affect (emotion). He describes the major neurochemical imbalances and deficits resulting from early deprivation. Both he and Dr. Schore have synthesized the results of many neurobiological and biochemical studies that relate to attachment and describe what can go wrong.

Dr. Daniel Siegel, from the UCLA School of Medicine, has written the best synthesized treatment of attachment and brain development. As someone "down stream" from Dr. Schore, Dr. Siegel has been able to expand on Dr. Schore's theories. Dr. Siegel has done a particularly outstanding job of examining the relationship between the left hemisphere's functions and the control center in the right hemisphere. While his approach to the brain is more modular and less hierarchical, Dr. Siegel has done a marvelous job explaining the synchronization of the brain based on development, memory, attachment style and mutual story telling.

Additional Sources

Dr. Daniel Amen has scanned over 80,000 human brains. As a psychiatrist interested in the brain's impact on emotion and personality and a practitioner of nuclear medicine, Dr. Amen has found brain patterns behind many common problems. His prolific writings, speaking, teaching and website www.brainplace.com are excellent sources of information on the brain. Dr. Amen proposes a wide variety of specific solutions, from diet to brain training, for each brain region he has studied. Dr. Amen has a fairly modular approach to the brain that provides clear and simple identification of activity levels associated with personality problems. His modules quite closely parallel the areas mentioned by Dr. Schore in his theories. Dr. Amen's work is excellent.

The advantage of Dr. Schore's hierarchical model over a modular one is that a hierarchy in the brain establishes both an order of brain development as well as the order in which brain functions break down if there are problems. For example, in the modular approach that Dr. Amen uses he will simply find out which modules are working and which are not and prescribe solutions for each. Dr. Schore's hierarchical model predicts that if the middle level (the cingulate cortex) is not working, the top level (orbitofrontal cortex) will also be impaired, as will the synchronization between hemispheres. You get more for your nickel with a hierarchical model.

Dr. Siegel, Dr. Antonio Damasio and Dr. Vilaynur Ramachandran all create brain models based on interactive modules. These non-linear models depend strongly on the activity of the reentry circuits described by Dr. Gerald Edelman. These are faintly hierarchical concepts. Dr. Guilio Tononi, however, dismisses modular approach entirely and depends instead on temporal synchronization and the brain's five chemical value systems for his explanations. These five chemical value systems are: dopamine, serotonin, epinephrine, norepinephrine and acetylcholine. These value systems are powerful in that they affect the responses of the brain in a global way when they are activated. These value systems feature prominently in Dr. Schore's hierarchical model that, like Dr. Tononi's, depends strongly on temporal synchronization for its explanations.

The work by Dr. Ronald A. Ruden and Marcia Byalick in *The Craving Brain* and that of Dr. Harvey Milkman and Dr. Stanley Sunderwirth in *Craving for Ecstasy* point to the importance of the nucleus accumbens in addictive behaviors. This part of the meso-cortical pleasure system in the basal ganglia attaches to both the orbitofrontal cortex and subcortical structures in Dr. Schore's model. Dr. Ruden discusses the interaction of the serotonin and dopamine value systems in the nucleus accumbens, while Dr. Milkman stays primarily with the dopamine system, with slight attention to the norepinephrine arousal needed for cravings. While neither of the books on cravings takes into account the central role of attachment in stimulation of pleasure and pain, Dr. Schore's theory makes both the pleasure and quieting functions of the pleasure/satiation system a direct product of attachment. Together with Dr. Siegel's explanation of how the brain manages not to know about its own pain, these writers provide a powerful model of how attachment failures produce the destructive cravings of badly bonded men.

Evidence would suggest that the emotional brain is synchronized internally at five levels, with primacy given to the right hemisphere at all levels except the fifth and highest (where the balance shifts based on our level of distress.) The first level is the attachment system in the deep limbic area. This level determines what and who is personal to me. It also determines my personal reality. Level one is strongly tied to the dopamine value system. The second level controls approach and avoidance, giving and receiving. This system, at the level of the amygdala, is tied to the epinephrine and norepinephrine value systems. With these two systems we control our alertness and action. The third level of synchronization involves the emotional energy levels and interpersonal reality in the cingulate cortex. This level synchronizes the brain internally and synchronizes with other minds externally. The cingulate cortex synchronizes the activity present in the different lobes of the brain as information is received and sorted. Level three can synchronize the activity of two minds into one point of view. This third level seems to synchronize serotonin and norepinephrine value systems associated with quieting and arousal. The fourth level of synchronization involves the direction of attention. Attention is the only resource humans have to offer. The orbitofrontal cortex at level four controls the serotonin system and, with it, the capacity to soothe and quiet the dopamine, epinephrine and norepinephrine arousal. Level four can synchronize the activity of three minds and three points of view. The fifth level of synchronization is between experience in the right hemisphere and explanations in the left. It is this synchronization that is tested by such methods as The Adult Attachment Inventory (AAI) and the TheoPhostic® process for addressing unresolved distress from the past that intrudes into current life.

The four level control center in the right hemisphere presented in the Life Model is a result of combining the work of these doctors. Not one of them can be said to agree with my four-level model, although Dr. Schore clearly established the top three levels in his hierarchy of the brain. In addition, our vision of hierarchically synchronized modules, shaped and conditioned by five value systems, would exceed what any one of them would propose. Dr. Schore and Dr. Siegel would certainly agree, however, that we have both individual and group minds and that synchronization is not just a matter of internal brain levels, but of interpersonal states of mind as well.

Erik Erikson's Developmental Stages

Erik Erikson developed a model of human growth that he divided into eight stages, each one with its own crisis. In the years since his observations were made, brain development studies have shown that the brain goes through profound growth changes during many of these stages. It is currently theorized that, during important transitions, the brain goes through a time of reorganization and then functions differently after that point. Without help from older brains, these transitions leave the newly transformed brain in a state of disorganization. Stages of development are physical, as well as mental and social.

Erikson's Eight Crises:

1. BASIC TRUST VERSUS BASIC MISTRUST: ages 0-1, I am what I am given. The infant's identity develops out of what he is given and how he is treated.
2. AUTONOMY VERSUS SHAME AND DOUBT: ages 1-3, I am what I will. The infant thinks of himself in terms of what he can do often, pulling his hand away and insisting on doing things himself.
3. INITIATIVE VERSUS GUILT: ages 3-6, I am what I imagine I will be. The child becomes the things and people he dreams he is. He loves to pretend and try new things.

4. INDUSTRY VERSUS INFERIORITY: ages 6-13, I am what I learn. The child begins to see that he must learn things he does not yet know. He sets out on quests, adventures, and conquests. Dreams become real.

5. IDENTITY VERSUS IDENTITY DIFFUSION: ages 13-19, I am all of the above. Each aspect of identity must be combined with the others to become an adult who contains all these attributes.

6. INTIMACY VERSUS ISOLATION: Young adult. He must now learn how to maintain himself in close harmony with others.

7. PRODUCTIVITY VERSUS SELF-ABSORPTION: Adulthood. He is now challenged to be the source of good things.

8. INTEGRITY VERSUS DESPAIR: Maturity. Now his soul must be capable of maintaining itself and his influence even if he loses some abilities and strength.

As can be observed, the LIFE Model stages generally combine two of Erikson's into one. There are several reasons for this. First, the categories we use — infant, child, adult, parent and elder are generally recognized across cultures and languages. Second, these are the categories mentioned in scripture. Third, our categories are usually used with the qualifier "young" by language, culture and scripture to indicate that those in the early part of the stage are different from those in the later part of the stage. So a *young man* is known to be different from a *man*.

Example:

LIFE Model	*Erikson's Crisis*	*Neurobiological*

INFANT STAGE

Infant 0-1	Trust versus Mistrust	Right Hemisphere Growth
Toddler 2-3	Autonomy versus Shame	Left Hemisphere Growth

WEANING - Reorganization of brain structure and identity

CHILD STAGE

Young child 4-6	Initiative versus Guilt	Rt. peak at 4, Lf. peak at 6
Child 7-12	Industry versus Inferiority	Rt. peak at 8, Lf. peak at 12

RITE OF PASSAGE - Reorganization of identity

ADULT STAGE

Young adult 13-17	Identity vs. I.D. Diffusion	Right Hemisphere Growth
Adult 18-24	Intimacy versus Isolation	Left Hemisphere Growth

BIRTH OF FIRST CHILD - Reorganization of identity and brain growth

The periods of right hemisphere growth are important as they constitute the best times for bonding, as well as for forming new identities. This observation is based on the right hemisphere's dominance for emotions, relationships and bonding. This is also where the most remediation can be done for existing bonding deficits. The best time to improve bonding, self-control, emotional expression and correct relational problems is during right hemisphere growth. During these times the right hemisphere may be more open to new experiences. These are the emotional intelligence development times. Conversely, verbal/logical development is best corrected or improved during left hemisphere growth. The times of left hemisphere growth are best for introspection and learning to speak about one's internal world to others.

PERIODS OF RIGHT HEMISPHERE GROWTH

AGE	STAGE	MAIN OBJECT
0-2 years	Early infant	Mother
4 years	Early child	Father
8 years	Late child	Friends
15 years	Early adult	Mate
First child	Early parent	Baby

It is important to note that the metamorphosis for the mind, body, and social development that occurs between stages will be attempted by the developing individual's brain based on an internal schedule. He or she is run by a biological clock as inexorable as the one that begins childbirth at about nine months. This means that each metamorphosis is attempted whether the child is being guided or has been abandoned. His attempts to grow continue even after an identity transformation fails. The child's capacity to live and mature will simply be diminished greatly from that point onward.

Writers, such as Harville Hendricks, have developed descriptions of what adults are like if they get stuck at one of these developmental crises. Hendricks particularly focuses on the effects which getting stuck produces in love relationships and mate selection. Notice the importance of this connection between the failure to grow up properly and adult life. Omitting or distorting any stage of development will produce a deficit in all the stages that come afterwards. Once again we see the power of a hierarchical model, this time of maturation. Further examples and tables can be found in this book.

As can be seen, these stages can be broken down into many smaller steps, accomplishments and developments such as Jean

Piaget has done with cognitive development or Kolberg has done with moral development. The five stages given in this book are sufficiently clear and useful for community use, although they do not include what is actually a sixth stage — prenatal. This sixth stage is the first in line. Counting the prenatal stage, man has a perfect six stages. As with the other five stages, the forty or so weeks of prenatal life also can be divided into substages or steps. That would be another book. The way we are made is awesome!

References

Allan N. Schore, *Affect Regulation and the Origin of the Self: Neurobiology of Emotional Development,* Hillsdale, NJ: Lawrence Erlbaum Associates Publishers, 1994.

Allan N. Schore, *Affect Regulation and the Repair of the Self,* New York, NY: W.W. Norton, 2003.

Allan N. Schore, *Affect Dysregulation and the Disorders of the Self,* New York, NY: W. W. Norton, 2003.

Erik H. Erikson, GROWTH AND CRISIS, in *Theories of Psychopathology and Personality* Edited by Theodore Millon, Philadelphia, PA: W. B. Saunders Co., 1973. Pages 136-156.

Bessel van der Kolk, *Psychological Trauma,* Washington, DC: American Psychiatric Press, 1987.

Daniel J. Siegel, *The Developing Mind: Toward a Neurobiology of Interpersonal Experience,* New York, NY: Guilford Press, 1999.

Daniel G. Amen, *Healing The Hardware of the Soul,* New York, NY: The Free Press, 2002.

Gerald M. Edelman, Guilio Tononi, *A Universe of Consciousness,* New York, NY: Basic Books, 2000.

Harvey Milkman and Stanley Sunderwirth, *Craving for Ecstasy,* San Francisco, CA: Josey-Bass Publishers, 1997.

Ronald A. Ruden and Marcia Byalick, *The Craving Brain,* New York, NY: Perennial, 2000.

Appendix D

Life Model Resources

r a

RA poppa y hoo . com